Recreating
Eden

The exquisitely simple, divinely ordained plan for
transforming your life and your planet

Julia Rogers Hamrick

New Realities Publishing
P.O. Box 24141
Denver, CO 80224
www.recreating-eden.com

ISBN 0-9749277-2-4
LCCN 2004102212

Design & Typesetting: The Roberts Group
Author Photo: Tanja Butler-Melone
Galaxy photo courtesy of HubbleSite

A note to the reader:
One of the main purposes of this book is to empower you to heed the authority of
your own Spirit above all other authority, including whatever authority my words
may seem to carry. What you read in this book is to be used solely as something
to consider in forming a reality model that works for you—not as advice. I trust
that you will take what resonates with you and leave the rest.

While I followed my inner guidance in choosing to go against standard medical advice, I don't advocate that you necessarily do likewise, but that you follow
only the path outlined by your *own* inner guidance with the input of whatever
health care professionals you are guided to consult.

Only *you* can determine what is the right course for you in any arena of your
life.

Recreating

Eden

Contents

DEDICATION

THIS BOOK IS DEDICATED TO THE ONE.

PREFACE

$\mathcal{W}$HEN I WAS TWENTY-SEVEN YEARS OLD, I found myself in a remarkable state of being I now understand was Paradise—the mythical Garden of Eden. While forays into extraordinary awareness are the goal of ascetics and other spiritual aspirants, in my case, I had not consciously aspired to this experience. In fact, I had never even realized it was a possibility! This radical and sudden elevation in consciousness had occurred not as a reward for spiritual discipline, but *spontaneously* as the end result of the simple thing I had done in response to finding myself in a situation I could not effectively deal with in the typical human way. When all else had failed, I turned my life completely over to God, and things snowballed from there.

As I will recount in more detail in the introduction, God had steered me to a natural healing clinic in Switzerland, from which I emerged radiant and healthy from a rapidly deteriorating physical condition. While there, I also experienced a spiritual healing, a literal and figurative mountaintop experience in which I transcended ordinary reality and briefly experienced cosmic consciousness. Even though it was only a moment or so before I reentered the familiar world, that all-too-brief, spontaneous sojourn into the realm of Paradise changed *everything*.

Thereafter, my reason for being was to develop a deeper spiritual understanding, and, as someone who has always been compelled to teach, to share with others whatever spiritual discoveries I was most excited about at any given time. Such was—and is—my greatest joy. In the background, however, there was always the nagging knowing that there was something vital I needed to share—and desperately *wanted* to share—but I just couldn't put my finger on what the message was to be. I was pretty clear that I was to write a book, but the exact contents and scope of the book were not yet for me to know.

I knew it had something to do with my experience in Switzerland, but the purpose of the book and its particulars seemed frustratingly nebulous. I frequently cried and pleaded with God to either show me what it was—or to let me off the hook from the responsibility of it. But neither of those things happened. Much of the time, I felt like a pregnant woman who was five or six years overdue, not really even sure what she was giving birth to!

During my quest to understand what message I was to be sharing, I was told by a prophet that within my experience in Switzerland was all the truth I would ever need for successfully living my life; that what I had gone through included exactly what I needed to know to fulfill my destiny. The story of my illness, with its pain and suffering; my grabbing hold of faith; my ascent to the Garden; and my tenure there—however temporary—as well as my "fall from grace" held the key not only to my personal redemption, but to the restoration of all humanity. The prophet pronounced that my mission in life was to teach people how to rejuvenate themselves.

I thought she was nuts. I accepted the part about my experience containing all the answers I would need for my life, but the rejuvenation bit—I thought maybe she had gotten her cosmic wires crossed and was talking about someone else! I wasn't the least bit interested in helping aging egomaniacs try to stave off the inevitable.

Only years afterward would I realize that she was precisely on target. She was not talking about the vanity aspect of rejuvenation, but about the *true* rejuvenation that occurs in the process of making your way back to Eden—indeed, the rejuvenation of the mind that is *necessary* in order to go back there. As the master teacher

Jesus proclaimed, "You must turn and become as a little child to enter the Kingdom of Heaven."

Indeed, I would come to understand that we must turn—shift our focus—and shed our sophistication and our baggage in order to open Eden's gate. As I continued my own process of spiritual growth, the puzzle pieces were gradually fitting together in my own mind, but I still couldn't understand exactly what I was expected to do. I just kept asking to be shown; most times, *begging* for clarification.

One day in 1995, as I sobbed out yet another plea to God to let me in on the plan, the proverbial lightning bolt struck me and I was at last able to understand some of the basics of the project before me—at least enough of them to get started. I did not at that time, however, grasp the enormity of what I was being asked to do: to explain how humanity first lost its home in Eden and, even more importantly, how it can deliver itself back to its original state, in complete harmony and oneness with the Whole of Creation, to reside in Eden once again. In retrospect, I see why I was kept in ignorance of this!

Instead of being shown the scope of the project or how things were to unfold, I was charged with the task of following my inner guidance, in the moment; to put down the ideas that came to me word by word. Sometimes they flowed—sometimes they didn't. I'd like to say I was completely cool with that, but the fact is that I responded with much consternation and self-flagellation for my not getting it done as fast as I thought I ought to be. After many years of this, it finally became clear that the pace of this project was completely out of my hands and that when you are doing the will of Heaven, you can pretty much count on not being able to call the shots!

Almost nine years later, I can tell you that, despite the frustration over the times when I didn't know what to do, the actual work on this book has, with few exceptions, been exhilarating. At the very same time I was writing, I was learning, never knowing for sure what I was about to type into the computer. Countless times I was surprised and utterly delighted with fascinating new insights I had never even considered until they showed up on the computer screen in front of me! That is how I could tell that this was not my project to steer at the human level—that there was clearly an intelligence much larger than Julia, the individual, in charge of it, drawing knowledge from a repository far greater than could fit in my personal brain.

At times the energy coming through me was so powerful, I could hardly contain it to get it translated into words. Many were the times I burst into tears of joy triggered by the strong energy rising in me as a new understanding presented itself. I suspect that this book's pages contain far more of that energy than the words can literally represent. For every page that is here, there were once three, maybe four times as many that did not make it past my internally guided editing. But I believe the electricity of those words is incorporated within the pages nonetheless and that the energy this book conveys is probably more potent than the words themselves.

I am profoundly and joyously grateful to have been given the task of putting this large piece of the human puzzle in place. While extraordinarily simple, and, in retrospect, almost glaringly obvious, it seems an enormous step in our collective understanding and is, perhaps, the matrix that the rest of the pieces of the puzzle are meant to plug into. I say this in all humility as this book and its elementary—yet revolutionary—concept has not been birthed of my own consciousness, but of a truth that has existed for millennia. I am merely the one who was called to the task of grounding it and nurturing it into this simple and easily understandable form.

You will find this book free of intellectual exercise or complex scientific or mathematical explanation. Indeed, I believe I was the right person for the job of putting forth this information precisely because of my lack of such leanings. My instruction throughout was to boil every concept down to the simplest common denominator and keep it free of complexity. It is clear to me that my tendency to see and express things in elementary terms has been perfectly suited to the task. This, combined with my immense love for Spirit, are what, I believe, qualified me to write this book. While there is no way to guarantee I got everything exactly right, I have done my best to scribe the understandings as accurately as possible.

It is up to you to discern the truth in the words and decide if they are helpful to you.

Make no mistake—while I do live this book's principles as closely as I can, and my life is all the more joyful because of it—I do not offer myself as an authority figure, and believe me, I am not yet listing Eden as my permanent address. I am simply a person who has had a glimpse of Home, is thrilled by what she has seen, and wants and needs a lot of company to help recreate Home right here on Earth. As an astute astrologer once told me, I am a path-leader—not because I am necessarily the most qualified to lead, but because I tend to run impatiently ahead on the path and get so excited about what I see, I am intent on running back and grabbing as many people as I can to make sure I have plenty of company with which to marvel over my discoveries!

That pretty much sums up how I perceive my role in this whole process of restoration. God-In-You is far more qualified to steer you in finding your own way back to Paradise and helping you create it on Earth, and that is who is to be your true leader. This book and I are just to serve as aids in remembering who you really are, why you are here, and how the very key to recreating the harmonious state of being you were designed to inhabit has been in you all the time—and, of course, to remind you how to use it to open Eden's gate.

Just as any proud mother, I have high hopes for this "child" I have birthed. Now that it is fully formed and ready to go out into the world to do its work, I send it forth with the prayer that it will reach its highest potential: helping to catalyze the shift in our collective consciousness that is necessary for transforming our world to one in which Love and harmony reign.

Julia Rogers Hamrick
April 2004
Denver, Colorado

Through the Garden Gate: A Glimpse of Eden

HAVE YOU BEEN TO PARADISE? Whether you can consciously remember it or not, I know you have—in fact, we *all* have. The Garden of Eden, the mythical Paradise of the Bible, is not a piece of real estate—it is a state of being. It is our "home" in the truest sense—it is our home of origin and our home of destiny. From the moment we departed from there, we have yearned to return, and though we've lost our way, that yearning has driven us throughout our lives. At the deepest level of our beings, we long to be completely free of stress and in harmony with all Creation the way we were intended to be—the way we were in the beginning. We long to be whole and fully energized with Life Force. We long to have everything provided for us the way it was in the Garden. We long to experience the pure joy and total ecstasy we remember from our beginnings.

Though most of us do not consciously associate all of the longings we experience with our primal need to return to our original state of being, it is present in everything we do. Despite having lost our way home, our motivation for everything in our lives—from our careers to our addictions, from our relationships to our spiritual quests, from our creative endeavors to our eating habits—stems from our deep, largely unconscious desire to return there; to once again inhabit the "Garden of Eden" and regain what we lost so long ago. Unfortunately, for the most part, we seek to fulfill our yearning for home in ways that will never really satisfy us.

Why do we crave intimacy and closeness? Because at our core, we know what real oneness is and we are programmed to seek it. Why do we strive for money and status? And why do we steal from others in large ways and in small, or disempower others with our thoughts, words, and deeds? Because we yearn to feel truly empowered and have forgotten where true power comes from and how to receive it. Why do we seek to get high from drugs? Because we know deep down what true ecstasy is and we're trying to achieve it—but in a fashion that will never provide it for us in any authentic or sustainable way. Why do we try to escape from stress by numbing ourselves with alcohol or food or television? Because we were not designed to live in stress and we are trying to recreate the state of no pain and no stress we are so desperately missing. Why are we lazy—or tempted to be—expecting something for nothing? Because we know at a deep level that we are, simply by the fact of our existence, supposed to be perfectly provided for without struggle the way we were in the Garden and we have forgotten how that really works.

We have forgotten that we can only experience what we are truly longing for by aligning ourselves with Source the way we were designed to be, and were in the beginning, so that we can have it all.

When we are again properly aligned with Source, we will feel that completeness, that wholeness again. We will no longer ache for the ease of our existence in the Garden, where our being-ness was all that was required of us—we will have it. We won't have to yearn for the experience of complete, unconditional, never-ending Love—we will be saturated with the perfect Love that is the sole medium in and upon which we exist in the Garden. We will no longer have to wait to feel total acceptance without having to prove anything—we will live in that state of grace. We will not feel deprived of power because we will channel immense power—*real* power—in ways that enhance all of Creation. We will no longer yearn to feel the ecstasy of union as we will be fully embraced in the experience of Oneness. We will be whole and fully energized again. We will live in bliss and total harmony—when we are fully aligned with Source once again the way we were created to be.

You are designed to be able to receive all the energy, abundance, power, wisdom, grace, and Love that Source has to offer—an infinite amount. In fact, before you were born, you were so perfectly aligned, you were in a state of total oneness with Source; you were bathed in ecstasy, and harmony was all you knew. But by being born on Earth, where the remembrance of our divine origins seems to be dim at best, you entered conditions that tended to separate you from your experience of Oneness and from your perfect alignment. Upon your arrival here, your attention was pulled away from Source and you became more fascinated with and reliant upon the world around you. You began to perceive yourself as separate—separate from others, and separate from Source—and thus, in effect, you are. That is why you are having to tough it out in exile from Paradise—while energy-depleted, no less.

There is only one way to receive Life Force, and that is through your alignment with the very source of it, but due to the loss of your perfect alignment with Source, you have received less and less of this necessary energy as you have adopted the ways of Earth-life. Without the full circulation of Life Force, your body and mind deteriorate, leading to, either sooner or later, physical death. But even more importantly, without full circulation of Life Force in and through you, you cannot *be* who you were created to be, *do* what you were created to do, or *have* all that you were intended to have. Because if you don't have this full circulation, it means that you are not fully aligned with the Source of Life Force—indeed, the Source of *All*—and when you aren't fully aligned, you are definitely outside of Paradise—sometimes *way* outside of it!

The time has come for this trend to be turned around. The good news I have for you is that, though you had a lot of help in doing so, *you exiled yourself*—and *you can re-admit yourself to the Garden at any time.* I did, which is how I know you can, too.

AT A CRITICAL JUNCTURE IN MY LIFE, having stumbled naively onto the Garden path, I was able to return, much to my surprise, to that rarefied state of being we're calling Paradise, if only briefly. Through a series of simple steps I took out of desperation, not knowing where they would take me, I found myself suddenly, unexpectedly, back in Eden. The power of that experience has shaped my life and driven me toward one outrageously ambitious and audacious goal ever since—to map the way so that everyone can find it and understand how it can—and *must*—manifest as a sustainable state.

The place was Switzerland; the time was December 1982. I was a twenty-seven-year-old American who had come to Zurich from Japan, where I was fulfilling an overseas-teaching contract, to enter a Swiss holistic clinic to which I had been guided. I needed help to heal myself from a critical, rapidly progressing case of rheumatoid arthritis, and to wean myself of the doctor-prescribed corticosteroids to which I had inadvertently become physically addicted. There were, as well, a battery of other strong, toxic medicines I had used in a failed effort to manage the excruciating pain and rapid deterioration of my body. Instinctively, I had felt they were killing me.

Having previously tried all that medical science had to offer me, and having gone from rheumatologist to rheumatologist, who offered me nothing but dire prognoses and medicines that didn't help, I finally realized in utter desperation that nothing outside of myself could save me. Terrified at the doctors' predictions of constant pain, wheelchairs, and a rapid decline leading to total disability, I naively called out to what I can best describe as the God of my Protestant, Sunday-school upbringing. I had always considered this god my "ace up my sleeve," and believed if I ever got desperate enough, I could call on "him" and he would help me. It was clear to me at that point that I was up against the wall and the time had come to exercise my last-resort option. The pleading voice that issued from me was that of a small child, calling for help from an omnipotent parent.

"Help me! Help me!" I sobbed over and over again until it

became an automatically repeating mantra that eventually dissolved into a primitive keening that went on for quite awhile. But after a time, the tears dried up, I became silent, and the "peace that passes understanding" enveloped me and quieted all my fears. I slept like a baby that night. The next day, I awoke feeling optimistic. *Very* optimistic! Immediately, I began receiving answers to my dilemma. They presented themselves in amazing ways along with easily workable solutions to what I had thought were impossible challenges.

This response made it clear to me that I had stumbled onto something incredibly powerful and that my best hope—my *only* hope—was in banking on this new way of approaching my problems. As I began to invest my trust in this god, I was rewarded with one astonishing result after another, and I found myself relying on God instead of my own intellect to figure things out and make them happen. The more I trusted and did the often illogical-seeming things I was guided to do, and saw that they paid off in magical ways, the more confident I was in putting my full trust in this obviously higher power. This trust, born out of stark terror, with all the options I had been able to come up with on my own having been exhausted, evolved into true, unshakable faith. In my observations since, I have become aware that desperation is often the birthplace of faith.

My new-found faith grew so strong, it became an almost tangible entity, and in my mind, there was nothing that could derail me from the God-filled path I was on. Whenever well-meaning friends and associates tried to interject *their* mundane reality into my impossible-seeming one of hope, miracles, and healing, I not only refused to entertain their doubts, I made no bones about refusing to even listen. I instinctively knew that if I was going to survive, I could only listen to the guidance within and that I had to tune out anything that conflicted with it.

I was absolutely certain that God was directing my every step and was assuring my success in finding the exit from the valley of the shadow of living death I had been inhabiting. I knew beyond doubt that putting my life in God's hands alone was my only viable choice. And God had brought me to Switzerland.

At the Swiss clinic, my recovery and rapid weaning from the

corticosteroids I had been living off of for many months astonished the doctors and nurses. Despite everyone's doubts that what I wanted to do was even possible, my faith guided me in rebelling from the doctors' advice and refusing all other medications in the process of getting off the cortisone. The wisdom within drove me to blaze my own trail to my body's deliverance. My inner guidance was infallible.

With help from the natural therapies offered at the clinic, including a cleansing, all-organic, vegetarian raw-foods diet, I was not only medication-free in record time, I began to thrive and was able to move freely and without pain for the first time in more than a year. Though they had originally held out little hope for me with my renegade methods, and had preached the certainty of doom for the course I had undertaken, my quick turnaround was, of course, termed a "miracle" by the medical experts who staffed both the clinic and the Zurich University Hospital. Suddenly I had many allies in those who had once been so dubious.

Through it all, my connection with God continued to strengthen. With each passing day, with each breath, I grew stronger spiritually as well as physically until I existed in an almost-giddy state of grace and harmony each and every minute. My faith was that of a child's—naively and completely trusting that God not only wanted me to be well but to grow closer and closer to "Him." I was rejuvenated at every level, and my joy knew no bounds.

One day while still at the clinic, I was feeling far better than I had in months—I had kicked the steroids and other medications, my symptoms were completely at bay, and indeed, I felt better than I ever remembered. I was in the mood for a bit of exploring and decided to go for a walk in the brilliant December sunshine and crisp Swiss air. The clinic was located at the foot of a small mountain, and I'd heard there was a fancy hotel at the top with a petting zoo. It sounded like a nice little adventure. The fact that I'd scarcely been able to walk when I'd arrived at the clinic just three weeks before was already a faded memory.

So I set off with great enthusiasm. It was such a glorious day, all was right with my world, and I felt as though I was walking on air. Even though I was not physically in shape for walking up such an unrelenting incline after almost a year of being crippled, somehow, every step energized me further. I was drawn toward the summit as if by magnetic force. My spirit was soaring.

I encountered other people on the way—some in their yards, some out walking, others driving by. After a few such encounters, I began to wonder if I looked as different as I felt. Everyone I passed or who passed me seemed to be staring at me. It wasn't a disturbing thing—in fact, I was enjoying it. I felt myself glowing and knew intuitively that the people were drawn to the energy that now seemed to be floating me along.

The higher I climbed, the more elated I became and the more electric my body felt. This rapidly expanding euphoria was unlike any phenomenon I remembered ever feeling before, and a tiny part of me wanted to resist the experience, but it was quickly overwhelmed by the tidal wave of joy that was increasing exponentially within me. I told myself to "just go with it" and so I did.

Everything I saw appeared to be glowing. More than just the brilliant sunlight that was striking them on the outside, they were lit from within. Edges were becoming blurred, and oddly, my sense of individuality was falling away. Even more oddly, it felt right! As I came to the top and reached the grounds of the hotel, my surroundings became so soft and so luminous, I felt that I was in heaven. My heart, expanding with every breath, seemed to be exploding and overflowing with pure love, filling every atom of my body.

I was drawn as if by a magnet to the outdoor petting zoo, deserted of people. The animals—goats, lambs, rabbits, ducks, and chickens—were all extraordinarily beautiful, and they were just as fascinated with me as I was with them. The boundaries separating us were rapidly becoming nonexistent, and the ecstasy building within me was so great it seemed to be expanding my cells to the bursting point.

A showy rooster with vivid plumage came to the fence and seemed to beckon me to him. As I drew close and gazed into the eye of this grand, feathered being, he seemed to be seeing right through my eye into my soul, and we connected at a level that utterly transcended our differing species. Rather than a barnyard animal, I saw within him an enormous and limitless universe. Suddenly, there was no distinction between us. We were one—not just with each other, but one with everything. It was as if his eye were a gateway, and in an instant, all that was physical fell away into a vast sea of pure Light where my only awareness was of utter bliss.

I would describe to you this "place" where I was, but there is no real description for it because when you are there, you are at one with it and unable to compare and contrast—you simply *are*. To have been able to observe it would have meant I'd have had to separate myself from it and once separated from it, *I simply would not have been there anymore.*

When you are in the awareness of Oneness, there is nothing—and everything—all at the same time. The closest I can come to explaining in retrospect what it was like is to compare it to the sensation I have known when newly in love—romantic love—*minus* any fears or doubts or human factors involved. Just the blissful, openhearted, spine-tingling, thrilling aspect of it. And still, that is a weak description as nothing I have ever known before or since can come close to the pure, ecstatic being-ness of my "mountaintop experience."

I don't know how long I remained in that state of total communion with the Oneness. In the realm of what I can now identify as what the mystics call "cosmic consciousness," there is no time as we understand it. All I know is that I would have gladly stayed forever if I could have, such was the ecstasy of that state of being. But I became aware of my insistent mind tugging at me, so eager to analyze and quantify the experience, and as I allowed my focus to shift back to my ordinary reality, things gradually redefined themselves so that I was once again cognizant of my body and my surroundings. The euphoria stayed with me, ebbing only gradually, as I walked back down the mountain, feeling so new, so transformed, so blessed, so awed.

I was, however, about to experience the excruciating pain of being in exile from Paradise.

While crossing a little footbridge just a short way from the clinic, another powerful surge of ecstatic energy came, and I found my steps slowing to make way for the awesome revelation about to explode in my mind. As I looked over the wooden railing to the icy creek below, the words came so distinctly and so powerfully, they nearly knocked me down.

"**I AM GOD.**"

It was not some large, booming man's voice but my *own inner voice* that had spoken so clearly. I was stunned and immediately overcome with shame. I was terrified of the audacity in my having proclaimed that. "What blasphemy! How dare I even consider such a thing? I am *not* God! No *person* is God! I am *so bad*," I thought.

Instantly all the energy that had built up in me over the last days and weeks drained from me as if sucked out by a vacuum cleaner. It was as if I were in an elevator on the hundredth floor of a skyscraper that suddenly fell back down to the ground and landed with a jolt. The feeling of connection I had had for months, the feeling of being held and supported by the hand of God had vanished in a second.

Where I had been full of vitality before, I now felt empty like a balloon with all its air let out, and I was suddenly very tired, my body aching as it hadn't since before I arrived in Switzerland. My lifeline seemed to have been severed, and for the first time since I had first cried out for help, I felt alone. Deeply alone and depressed. What had I done? It would take me years to discover the answer in its fullness.

The following chapters are dedicated to sharing my answer to that with you, as well as a simple strategy for all of us to achieve and sustain the amazing state of harmony I found on the way to the top of that mountain in Zurich—and ultimately, to reside in complete Oneness again.

IMAGINE IF EVERYONE WERE TO REALIGN THEMSELVES WITH SOURCE to receive a full flow of Life Force, of Love, in and through them so that they were saturated with it. Imagine if everyone were completely at ease, fulfilled, empowered, whole, blissful. There would be no war. There would be no violence. There would be no greed. There would be no stealing. There would be no lack. There would be no abuse. There would be no suffering. There would be no disharmony at all. It would be Paradise on Planet Earth. And it is entirely possible for us to create it.

Because Earth is a process-oriented planet—witness the process of birth, the process of growth, the *process of transformation*—creating Paradise here is a process, too. And while not so long ago I would have said that this process will take a long time and that it is unlikely it will be completely accomplished in our lifetime, I'm not at all sure of that anymore. Something astounding is unfolding, and a window of opportunity like none before has opened for the transformation of Earth and her citizens. A wave of energy such as we've never experienced is making our every loving intention in this direction pregnant with the promise of manifestation.

The time has come for Earth to be restored to harmony, and there are powerful forces conspiring to make it so—making this new Eden a reality is Priority One for the many forces of Light in our universe. For our part, all we must do is commit to making the simple but powerful changes in our own lives that will revolutionize our experience and, in the process, raise the planet up.

While consistently living in Paradise may seem hard to fathom given the way things are, and indeed, given our ego-resistance to giving up that which is more familiar, we merely need to *begin* to create a new world where Earth is as close to Heaven as possible, and the momentum of this will set in motion a transformation, both personal and planetary, that is unprecedented in our experience. As this book progresses, you will see just how this can be.

In fact, the very task we have vowed to undertake by being born in this period of time is that of bringing the Paradise experience to bear on this planet and making it a reflection of our true home in the Heart of God. Our mission is to make Earth a realm where the hallmarks of Paradise are present, even as we remain individuated human beings; to make it a reality where our consciousness and our behaviors reflect our origins in Eden more and more.

You may already be aware that this is your task and have traveled a ways on the path back to the Garden, whether or not you fully realized it was Paradise you were seeking to recreate. So you already know how much better life can be almost immediately once you totally commit to heading Home. If this seems to be a new concept to you, I want to assure you that it really isn't—you just need a little jog to your deep, encoded memories of Eden and of your pledge to return to it. This book will serve as that.

Though it is surely obvious that Planet Earth and her citizens are at a critical point in evolution and change is imminent, this undertaking is not purely an altruistic mission—no, not at all. The fact of the matter is that only when your own life is one of joy and fulfillment can the collective goal of renewing our planet be achieved. And getting to joy and fulfillment is not the long process we have believed it was!

What we have overlooked till now is that because of the way we are designed, it actually takes far more energy and work to stay outside the bounds of Eden than it does to return! By coordinating with our Creator's design for us, we are on the fast track to a new life. No longer does this need to be an arduous, s-l-o-w process of *working* on yourself—unless you want it to be! I don't know about you, but *I* have just about had it with the "Struggle School of Transformation"! Been there, done that, and none-too-impressed with it. You, too, I bet.

What I am announcing to you is a new era—a whole new opportunity for rapid growth and real, deep change, with untold benefits on the way. Like I did in the magical weeks and months leading up to my "mountaintop experience," we can live in a state of grace and increase the harmony in our lives so that even the greatest challenges are easy to deal with—or more accurately, so that the challenges are fewer and fewer. We can bring the characteristics of Home into our lives more and more, even as we maintain our individuality and personality—though I must warn you, it is likely that your personality will be transformed and made more delightful and magnetic as the process moves forward!

Though this road we've been on that has lead away from Source has been hard and heartbreaking, we are, after all, human beings, with all the necessary equipment for perceiving ourselves as separate and operating that way, even if it is a very tough way to exist.

The Creator makes no mistakes; so apparently, we were *destined* to leave the Garden. It's just that it is high time now to turn around and draw closer to Source once again, closer to the Garden. It is time to allow bliss to call us back to our origins. And with the promise of exponentially increasing energy, harmony, and joy, the trip back Home will be a glorious one!

I know that comes as a relief for those of you who are thinking, "Well, Paradise on Earth is an interesting concept but I'm not ready to live in a world where there is no contrast, no challenge, no work or individual recognition, and certainly not one where there is no need for sex!" Worry not—this first leg of the journey simply brings more exciting contrast, more thrilling challenges, more meaningful work, and dare I say it—more ecstatic sex!

It will bring more fulfilling relationships, more true prosperity, greater accomplishment, and a healthier body. The farther you travel on the path back Home, the more consistently joyful will be your experience. And worry not—as you draw closer, the releasing of your attachment to the old, familiar—but limiting—forms will not only be natural and far easier than you can imagine, your embrace of Oneness will be your greatest desire. It is in your very design.

Life was never supposed to be difficult. We have made it so by operating in ways we were never designed to. By making a simple change in the way you approach life, in the way you operate, you can tap into the magic of aligning with your design to rapidly transform your life and create your own paradise. And once you are in the process of doing so, you will *automatically* be a key player in transforming Planet Earth back into the paradise it once was and is destined to be again.

So let's get going. There is much I need to share with you and no time to delay!

CHAPTER ONE

Leaving Paradise: Growing up on Earth

*I*N THE BEGINNING, YOU WERE PERFECT. As a newborn, you were fresh from the Garden, radiantly alive, perfectly aligned with Source, and fully equipped to mature into an unlimited being of great spiritual power, leading a fulfilled life of creativity, joy, and harmony. No matter the circumstances into which you made your debut on Planet Earth, or into whose charge you were delivered, you arose from Divinity and began your existence as a dynamic expression of your Creator's great love for Life. You were born to be a flawless reflection of your Creator and to act as your Creator's representative in the world, blessing it with your Love.

So from this state of perfection and great promise, how did you become the all-too-frequently stressed-out, weary, disheartened person that you are now? How did you forget who you really are and why you are here? How did you lose touch with your unique abilities and natural rhythms? Why are you so inconsistently able to channel the divine Love you came to Earth to impart? From whence does your deep anger and sadness come? What caused you to leave Paradise? How did you wander so far from Eden?

As with most dramatic stories with happy endings, before we can get to the exciting, uplifting part, we first need to see how the protagonist gets in trouble before we discover how he or she will be saved. I feel sure you would like to know what happened to drive the main character in your own story—you—out of Eden. So before we see how you will make your triumphant return to the magnificent state of being you were designed to inhabit, we're going to start by looking at the forces that conspired to make you the wounded human you've become and that put you where you are today, living in a reality that is not reflective of your origins in the Garden.

EACH OF OUR PARTICULAR SITUATIONS IS DIFFERENT, and our stories are as varied as our circumstances, but the causes of our basic wounds are the same and as universal as our humanity. As you read through this chapter, it will be helpful to apply the general concepts presented within it to your own, very personal experience of growing up; to view your own story in light of the ideas presented herein. Some of us had more pleasant experiences than others, but regardless of our perceptions of this pivotal period in our lives, *all* of us underwent Earth indoctrination and became separated from our original state of wholeness. Even those whose upbringing would appear to be ideal could not help but be affected by the dysfunctional energy patterns pervading humanity and be altered by them.

Although you very likely experienced many happy times in childhood, and indeed, I truly hope you did, in this chapter my emphasis will *not* be on the more pleasant aspects of this part of your life or on the many constructive influences you encountered during your upbringing. It will not be on all the things your parents probably did right. Instead, my aim here is to help you understand that, because of the unhealthy patterns prevailing here on Earth, your basic wounding, disempowerment, and disconnection from the paradisiacal state was a given.

It is vital that you be willing to look at your past and your up-bringing with an objective eye, to allow yourself to take a step back and see through the family mythology and be able to acknowledge that just as *no* human being is perfect, neither were your parents or other caretakers. It is also mandatory to understand that the reason no human being on Planet Earth is perfect is that we are *all*, without exception, recipients of the legacy of dysfunction that has been passed down from generation to generation.

Just as important as seeing things clearly and dispassionately is getting past the point of blame and resentment toward your parents for their imperfections and their imperfect ways of relating to you. That is paramount for making it to the kind of understanding that is required for freeing yourself of the baggage of your growing-up period so that you can walk the path back to the Garden unencumbered. Indeed, you cannot pass through the Garden Gate unless you are willing to leave your "stuff" behind.

Exploring the dynamics of your upbringing is not so you can dwell on it, but so you can learn what you need to in order to get on with your purpose for being here. While we need to acknowledge what happened to wound us, focusing too intently on what happened in your past and thrashing about in the pain of it can be a wide detour. Instead of being helpful, it can delay your progress. It is up to you to be attuned with your inner guidance to determine what amount of examination of your past is therapeutic and purposeful, and when it becomes a trap that keeps you from moving on. For our purposes, it is simply important to see that what happened in your upbringing is why you have lost touch with the truth of who you are and how you were designed to be. *Be assured that this is true of every one of us.*

This chapter is basically about your early life—the way it was meant to be but wasn't, and why; and the way it was instead and why. It is designed to help you view it objectively instead of subjectively the way most of us regard our early years. It is intended to show you that you couldn't possibly have helped how you turned out. But it is also to show you that you must now use your awareness to rise up out of this dysfunctional past to create a present and future that better reflect who you really are and that help you return to the blissful state you are meant to inhabit.

If the following general story of your origins doesn't fit with your current view of who you are or how you came to be, or with your current understanding of who and what God is, please just read this as an allegory that will act as a bridge to the main concepts of this chapter that will surely resonate with you. In upcoming chapters, I'm going to be explaining and elaborating on the concepts I'm about to present to you. So without further ado, The Sad Story of You . . . and Me . . . and the Rest of Us.

BEFORE YOU BEGAN TO GROW YOURSELF A HUMAN FORM in your mother's womb, you were as powerful as it is possible to be. In effect, "you" were not "you," but simply a nondifferentiated aspect of God, of Great Spirit, completely unified with your Source, enjoying the state of total oneness and ecstasy. When the impulse arose within this Great Spirit to express as "you," your Spirit individuated, like a wave being created in the ocean, still an integral part of the ocean yet distinct and individual at the same time. Your Spirit was magnetized to the parents who could provide you with the genetic characteristics and environment that best served the purposes of the Creator.

Through the union of this man and woman during sex, an energy pathway was created by which your Spirit could enter the womb of your mother and implant the blueprint for your physical being. Once in place, the matter needed to create your body-mind began to form around this template according to its encoded instructions. In a healthy world, the rest of your development would have gone something like this: From the moment of your conception in the womb, you would not only have been provided with the physical elements you needed to grow a perfect body, but you would have been continuously bathed in totally loving vibrations. When your body had reached its optimal development within the uterus and you were ready to emerge, you would have been welcomed into your new reality—a world of harmony—with gentleness and great joy.

Your parents and the other adults in your experience would have been completely healthy, fully self-aware, wholly radiant individuals who understood who they truly were and the purpose they had come to the planet to serve. They would have been totally devoted to supporting your perpetual remembrance of your divine origins, and would have made the maintenance of your obedience to your inner guidance—and *not* to external authority—their prime parental objective.

You would have been continually empowered by these others, and your individuality and unique gifts not only encouraged, but celebrated. The natural flow of your energy would have been honored, and you would have been supported in doing *whatever* felt right for you, *whenever* it felt right. Your actions would always have been appropriate and productive because you would have been highly attuned with Spirit and thus in harmony with the Whole of Creation, and the need for correction from your caretakers would have been minimal, consisting simply of reminders to listen more closely to the guidance within and obey *it*—not them.

Of course, in the world the way it was originally designed to operate, your parents would have had an abundance of time and energy to spend with you, and helping you grow would have constituted their greatest pleasure. In this Eden, where everything would have been supplied because of perfect obedience to God, hard work would have been unnecessary. Your parents, living a stress-free existence, would have had infinite amounts of patience and, as perfect reflections of the Creator, would have been unconditionally and continually loving. You would never have had to "act out" to gain energy in the form of attention, because you would have had all the energy, attention, and love you needed. Your childhood would have been an experience of ever-increasing joy and fulfillment.

In such an atmosphere of total acceptance, the vast amounts of Life Force flowing through you would have stabilized in healthy patterns, and you would have matured into a radiant being of great power. You would have emerged from your youth even more energized than when you were born—balanced, aware, and fully prepared to play your unique role in the outworking of the Creator's

Plan with ease—and, of course, to do your primary job, which is to be a flawless transmitter of Love to all the world.

So what happened instead? Why was childhood so painful? Why is adulthood so trying? The answer is simple: You were *not* born into a healthy world—you were born into a world of wounded humans who were operating contrary to the Divine Design and, thus, were not even close to being in complete harmony with the Whole of Creation. In this environment, there was virtually no chance that you could remain whole and attuned with the truth of who you are or learn to coordinate with your design to achieve true success. By the time you had run through your first dozen diapers, you were well on your way to becoming a wounded human, too.

Earth, you see, is rife with influences working against the preservation of your wholeness and knowledge of your true identity. Strong currents of harmful energy (which we will learn more about soon) tend to affect whatever they come in contact, with and unless whatever they contact is consciously aligned with Source, it is damaged. As a newborn, not yet having come to full consciousness in the human state, you were especially susceptible to the influences surrounding you. From the moment of your conception in the womb, you were immersed in the harsh patterns of clashing energy currents prevailing on Earth. Over time, those currents would do quite a number on you.

YOU WERE, AT THIS BEGINNING POINT OF YOUR LIFE IN A HUMAN BODY, what we will call your *Original Self*, the optimal version of you *in potential*. Had your environment supported it, you subsequently would have developed into the optimal version of you—the mature version of your Original Self we'll call your true self—your Self with a capital "s." You would have reached that potential to become the fully empowered, spiritually focused human being you were meant to be, masterfully playing your part in the Divine Design, experiencing constant harmony and perfect fulfillment.

But since you were born into a world that was not at all conducive to that, and since your caretakers were hardly in a position to

LEAVING PARADISE: GROWING UP ON EARTH

teach you how to become a master of humanity and a steward of Heaven on Earth, you did not receive the guidance and environmental support you needed to achieve this. Your parents did not guide you in this because they did not know how to, having never received that guidance from their own parents. And most likely, through no fault of their own, they were pretty much clueless about their true nature and did not even know about their own divine identity, much less yours!

You see, they, too, had undergone the process of separation that has been the sad plight of nearly everyone who has been born on this planet. Their human experience, just as yours would be, had been dictated in large measure not only by their own wounded and misguided parents, but by a whole mixed-up civilization that had long ago been created by human minds generating the chaos that manifests when minds operate without the constant guidance of Spirit.

This civilization that your parents were born into—as well as their parents and grandparents and *their* parents and grandparents before them, back for hundreds of generations—promulgated the false notion that humans are *separate* from God as well as separate from everyone else. This civilization fostered the belief that external authority, not internal authority, must rule, essentially leaving little room for honoring the voice of Spirit within. So, lacking the knowledge of their own divine natures and having been indoctrinated in such a way that they basically gave up their direct communication with God to make their way in the world, your caretakers were not able to help you maintain yours.

It is important to establish up front that your caretakers did the best they could with the limited understanding they had, regardless of anyone's opinion of their character or parenting skills. They gave you as much love, attention, and nurturing as they were capable of, whether or not it was enough. They took care of you to the best of their abilities as the wounded human beings they were. The kind of parents your parents turned out to be is the product of how they, themselves, were parented. How they related to you had everything to do with how their own wounded parents had related to them. How they were made to feel about themselves is highly relevant to the way you now feel about yourself. Their capacity to love you, and the way they were able to demonstrate that love to you, was greatly impacted by the amount of love and quality of nurturing *they* had received and the way they experienced it.

Regardless of how much love your parents were able to give you, who you are now is in large part the result of the dysfunctional legacy they received from their own parents and have, in turn, passed on to you. Because of the state of things here on Earth, even the most caring, affectionate, generous, and well-meaning parents have not been able to be the unconditionally loving representatives of the Divine they were intended to be. Life on this planet has taken its toll on them—just as it has taken its toll on you. Like every human since Adam and Eve left the Garden, your parents had been strapped with that ancient legacy of dysfunction passed down from generation to generation.

This bequest consists not only of limiting belief systems developed from the painful experiences of those who have gone before, but even more elementally, it passes on those ideals and practices which are at the very root of humanity's pain—the pain born of being separated from Source and from the truth of who you are. What you receive from all the humans who have gone before is the false notion that God's voice sounding within you can be ignored—even disobeyed—with impunity, and that you are separate from God and the rest of Creation. This "legacy of dysfunction" originated in the event that is described by the *Holy Bible*, and a myriad of other religious texts, as the Fall of Man from the Garden of Eden, and has passed from human to human down through the ages ever since. In chapter 3, we will examine The Fall more closely.

FOR AS FAR BACK AS ANYONE CAN REMEMBER, the process of growing up on Planet Earth has required making a shift from a total reliance and focus on the divinity which is innate within you, to a reliance on externals. This systematic process of disempowerment that begins the moment you are born is initiated as a result of your being dependent on your parents for your very survival. Although the appointment of your parents as your caretakers and providers for the first years of your life is an important part of the Creator's design, out of a lack of understanding it becomes the beginning of your tragic separation from the full awareness of and obedience to your own inner guidance—God's voice sounding within you.

Because, as a human infant, you had not yet developed the physical capacity to survive on Earth, your parents were provided to maintain you until—and *only* until—such time as you could maintain yourself. They were designated to act as special agents of the Creator, to embody for you the qualities of Mother God and Father God, and to be your models of what radiant human beings can be. They were given the responsibility of teaching you how to maintain your perfect alignment with Source and how to do the job you had come to Earth to do. Had they, themselves, been fully aligned with Source, they would have understood this, and would have easily been able to carry out this important mission.

If they had been able to perform the most important aspect of their assignment—to help you stay focused on and aligned with your Spirit—they would never have allowed you to mistake them as being your ultimate authorities and primary sources of sustenance. They would have made sure you knew that they were merely your guardians and teachers, and that your Spirit is your only true authority and lifeline to Source. But, as we've already seen, they were wounded humans, not the perfect reflections of Spirit they were intended to be. They didn't understand the true nature and purpose of the job with which they had been entrusted.

Instead, they believed that their major duty as your parents was to guide you and control you—even dominate you—until you had taken on enough of the "do's and don'ts" of the world around you so that you could use these guidelines to control yourself. They had been indoctrinated to believe that they *must* control you if they were to train you properly in the ways of civilization. Making sure you conformed with the structure, values, and customs of society was, in their minds, the key to preparing you to survive on your own.

Of course, even in a healthy world, *some* parental control over small children is, indeed, necessary to assure that no physical harm

9

comes to them, and that they cause no harm to others. After all, with such high levels of energy coursing through them and physical bodies that have not yet developed fully enough to consistently control themselves, children are predisposed to calamity without some external control. So the Creator has provided for that by giving babies parents to watch over them. But the problem arises when, instead of assisting children in developing *Spirit-centered control from within,* parents continue to control them from without.

One reason they do so, aside from the belief that they are *supposed* to, is that it feels good to them. It is important to understand that for your caretakers, who had felt powerless to some degree ever since they transferred *their* primary allegiance from God-In-Them to their *own* parents, having you subject to their control may have offered them their first sense of power since infancy. After having been at the mercy of others for so long, it is understandable that they, innocently, would try to regain a feeling of power through controlling you just as they were controlled.

No one can control you unless you fear what will happen if you don't allow them to. Fear is the chief commodity of control—without it, no one can control another. Both as a helpless baby at the mercy of less-than-perfect parents, and also as an adult, your primary fear is that you will not get your needs met, and this makes you vulnerable to being controlled. Such fear, of course, stems from not knowing that your every need will be provided for by relying on Spirit wholeheartedly and exclusively—the way you did before you left the Garden. Based on the condition of your caretakers, it is easy to see why you would come to be concerned about this!

The fear of not getting your needs met not only makes you vulnerable to being controlled by others, it also causes you to come up with your own control strategies—the type developed by those who perceive themselves as being without overt power. When you, a defenseless infant without the physical ability to provide for yourself, found yourself totally reliant on these wounded adults, you quickly figured out how you must behave in order to assure that they would meet your needs for food, shelter, affection, and stimulation.

This was necessary because your parents were frequently distracted from the job at hand. Unlike the deity they were intended to act as extensions of, they were *not* able to provide for you effort-lessly and unconditionally. They had to work at it. They had to interact with and manipulate the world around them (basically, to do what they needed to do to please other humans, just as you were learning to please them) so that they could meet not only their own survival needs but yours, too, something which they were not really equipped to do. This is a very stressful way to operate when you are designed to be effortlessly provided for by your Cre-ator! So, impacting their ability to care for you were their own, very human issues and struggles; therefore, you had to come up with ways to get their attention and to please them.

Thus, you learned to do whatever evoked a response that pro-cured you whatever you needed, even if doing what it took to please them and assure their approval was not in alignment with the flow of energy within you. In other words, just as the legions of human beings before you had done, *you gave up your divine right to behave as your inner impulses guided you to in exchange for your so-called safety and security in the world.* And to a large de-gree, you have been doing that ever since. Using behavioral strat-egies to get your caretakers to meet your needs was the beginning of an ongoing pattern of manipulation on your part, albeit born of innocence. Once you learned that you could get what you needed from them by modifying your behavior, it became one of your basic tools for survival in the world at large where you con-tinued to perceive your well-being to be completely dependent on the good will of other humans.

To expand upon the understanding of what your parents were deal-ing with while they were rearing you and how that affected your development, let's look at how some of your deepest wounds re-sulted from your parents' struggles. Because of their own indoctri-nation to the ways of the, shall we say, "wacked-out world," and their pattern of relying on their own mental abilities to steward their actions, your parents were functioning in a manner that as-sured them ongoing difficulty. Whether they were doing whatever they thought would please their boss, their spouse, or the public-at-large, they were having to act counter to their true natures even though they may not have even realized it.

As we will soon look at more closely, giving your primary allegiance to externals aligns you with conditions, situations, and people that are out of harmony with the Whole, magnetizing chaos and stress. So, your externally focused caretakers, with their drive to succeed according to societal standards and operating without the benefit of the guiding intelligence of Spirit, were under a great deal of strain just trying to make their way in the world. The frustration of their difficulties naturally affected the amount of energy and patience they had for you.

Training you, a little dynamo filled to the brim with Life Force and driven by powerful inner urges and impulses, to deny your nature and conform instead to the dictates of an externally focused civilization was a tough job—it takes a great deal of stamina and persistence to impose an unnatural order on a natural being. Assign such a mammoth task to already energy-deficient, stressed-out parents, and add to this the deep-seated pain they have been carrying since their own childhoods, and you have a recipe for hurtful interaction, with you on the receiving end. This is how abuse is spawned.

The attempt by adults to feel more energized, empowered, and in control often results in abuse of their children. Child abuse doesn't just consist of the more drastic forms we normally consider to be abuse, such as hitting, inappropriate sexual contact, or other physical and emotional violations, but includes *all* attempts by adults, whether conscious or unconscious, to re-empower themselves by disempowering children. Even if yours were the most caring and well-meaning parents on Earth, they very likely indulged in *dis*empowering you from time to time by somehow implying their superiority as parents and your inferiority as a child.

Criticism, faultfinding, belittlement, and displays of exasperation (be they through a well-placed sigh or a fit of yelling) are commonly employed techniques for making parents feel superior and, in the process, sapping children's energy. Though seemingly nonviolent, these practices can be classified as verbal and emotional abuse and have the potential to cause as much harm and pain as does abuse with a physical component. Although this kind of frustration-release produces a *temporary* rush of energy for the controlling parent, it is not satisfying for long, and tragically, it produces *lasting* damage to the child's psyche. The saddest part is that if we were properly aligned with Source—the source of all power—the way we were designed to be, we would never need to try and reenergize ourselves this way because we would be filled with authentic power.

So while it is horrific, and needs to end (along with the whole pattern that precipitates it), the abuse heaped upon us as children is understandable, if indefensible. You must realize that your very presence, so full of life and as yet so unaffected by society's rules, pushed all kinds of buttons in your parents. You reminded them, at the subconscious level, of their own Original Selves and the painful process of being separated from that state of bliss. Not only that, they were being forced by the mandates of society to impose upon you the same tragic exile from Eden that they had gone through, and they may have allowed their pain and anger relating to all this to bubble to the surface, with you the unwitting target.

With your circuits wide open as they were, it didn't take much to harm you—even the slightest careless remark or expression of irritation may have been recorded in your psyche as a comment on your worthiness as a human being. Your parents' faces were your mirrors, and whatever showed on them was how you saw yourself. You were tender and vulnerable as a child, and you did not understand that your parents' rage and exasperation had little to do with you, but primarily to do with their own inner struggles. You took everything personally, and because you didn't know what else to do with it, you stored the resulting pain deep within your being, and there it has stayed, to be reactivated over and over again. It is time to see things for what they are, and let that pain go. As the process of moving closer to Eden unfolds, this will become natural and easy.

THE PROCESS OF LEARNING TO SUBMIT TO EXTERNAL AUTHORITY and conform to what amounts to a perceptual overlay of "shoulds," "oughts," and "supposed-tos" designed by the human mind is not only painful, it is also confusing, especially when you are still so closely attuned with your inner world. To adhere to such a set of rules requires you to virtually disregard the moment-to-moment instructions and impulses arising from your own all-wise Spirit. As a child, your only incentives for this are pleasing your caretakers or avoiding their wrath, and until enough consistent effort, pressure, and, sometimes, even force is applied by the adults in charge, these external motivations are not much of a match for your powerful internal drive.

You must learn, for example, to eat when it is mealtime instead of when you are hungry, to sleep when it is bedtime instead of when you are sleepy, to be silent even though sound is welling up in you, to stop crying even though the tears are springing forth, and to be still when waves of energy are surging through you, demanding to be expressed. Basically, this training program requires you to act even when you are not motivated from within to do so, and to refrain from acting even though the voice within is telling you to act. Instead of being free to obey your body's own natural energy flow and the impulses and instructions coming from your Spirit, you must learn to obey, instead, the mandates of your parents, and, eventually, to conform to the structure and mores of society at large.

Your parents aren't alone in their task of teaching you to deny your internal authority so that you can be obedient to authorities outside of yourself. They have powerful reinforcements to assist them, especially our educational system. Once you reach school age and spend much of each day in the classroom learning the rules in a more formal way, the process is accelerated. Though there are some blessed exceptions, all in all, our schools are designed in such a way that obedience to the wisdom within is not reinforced nor celebrated. Spirit-guided wisdom is ignored in favor of assimilating information from external sources and conforming to "norms." All too many times, the students' natural proclivities are abandoned in favor of what will supposedly lead to external success with the promise of material prosperity. No wonder so many of us struggle in school and wake up in mid-life to discover that the career path we have followed has little to do with our passions and true talents! Abandoning your innate talents, abilities, and rhythms to fit into the world the way it is is the path to ultimate disempowerment—*any time you divorce a being from its natural state, it is at a major disadvantage.* When you are without the freedom to be who you are designed to be, the flow of Life Force within you is diminished, and you are, necessarily, less powerful. And, of course, without the liberty to obey the guidance of your Spirit, you are destined to operate out of harmony with the Whole, thus creating a frustrating existence of constant stress.

Although our parents' influence remains a powerful force throughout our lifetimes, for most of us, the time spent under their *direct* control ends sometime in late adolescence or early adulthood. To prepare you for this, you were programmed from early childhood to understand that, upon your maturity, you were going to go out into the world on your own. But when this occurred, it did not mean freedom; it meant even greater stress. Unfortunately, your parents brought you up to believe that once you withdrew your dependency from them, you were to *transfer* your trust to your own human abilities to cope in the world.

They convinced you that you must learn to depend on the resourcefulness of your own mind and your competence to fit into society. Thus, all efforts to prepare you to survive after leaving the nest were directed toward that end, and you embarked on adulthood with tools that were supposed to help you succeed in the externally focused world, but with little or no awareness of Spirit's ability to steward your life in joy and harmony—the *one* thing that could ensure your *true* success.

That, my friend, is truly tragic.

Sadly, as you can see, you had little choice but to develop the very patterns that would assure your deterioration. By now it is probably clear to you that the deck was stacked against you from the start. With so many forces working counter to your being able to maintain a total dependence on and trust in your Spirit, you had virtually no chance of remaining true to your design, maintaining your natural energy flow, and preserving your wholeness.

The process of growing up on Earth was a course in developing the habits that keep you from being totally aligned with Source for a constant supply of Life Force. It was instruction in how to stay *out* of harmony with the Whole of Creation, the very state that would have brought you the stress-free paradisiacal state you were meant to experience throughout your life. It was a course in forgetting who you really are and why you are here. It was, harshly but accurately stated, a death sentence.

I believe that this is the root cause of your deepest anger and your greatest sorrow. Beneath your conscious remembrance of your childhood—whether it was mostly happy or mostly unhappy at its surface—and beyond all the specific events that happened to wound you is the primal pain of your forced separation from the truth of who you are and from the way you were designed to function for *true* success as a human being.

Now that you've seen how the person you are now was shaped by so many unhealthy influences beyond your control, you may be tempted to claim victim status, throw up your hands, and wallow in self-pity. Okay. Go ahead and take about five minutes to do that— then you'd better snap out of it so you can get on with the task at hand. The knowledge of how you became less than who you were created to be is not a license to dig more deeply into dysfunction, but instead, is a tool for making your way out of it.

Yes, this is the job ahead of you—to acknowledge the limitations you have taken on in your upbringing, for whatever reason, and then to transcend them and recreate your life according to your divine origins. And even though others played major roles in shaping you before, it is solely within your power to restore your life to what it was meant to be and make your way back to Eden.

And here's a little extra food for thought: What if, while all the foregoing is true, you were *not* actually the victim in all this? What if, prior to your incarnating in a human body and joining the Earth family, you—your Spirit—chose to experience what growing up on Earth is currently about so that you could participate in a revolution—the revolution that, among other things, busts the "victim" dynamic and causes it to cease to be? If you *chose* to experience it, then you aren't truly a victim, now are you? Regardless of whether this is the case or not, I am absolutely sure that your mission now is to break out of the victim dynamic and participate in the revolution of the mind that leads to the recreation of Eden.

So when you're finished grieving the loss of your perfect alignment with Source and your personal departure from Paradise and are ready to move into the "It's time to *do* something about this" phase, let's look more closely at the great Divine Design and how you are engineered to fit into it. Then we'll see how all the trouble on Planet Earth began.

CHAPTER TWO

Prime Principle:
The Law of Harmony

*T*O UNDERSTAND THE SIMPLE BUT POTENT STEPS you will need to take in restoring yourself from the wounded human you've become to the kind of radiance you were designed to embody, it is important to have a rudimentary understanding of some of the larger dynamics of our universe and how it works. Being able to intentionally coordinate with the Creator's design for harmony and the laws that govern your world—not the man-made laws, but the natural ones that determine how things play out here on Planet Earth—will greatly expedite your progress toward a life of ever-increasing bliss. These laws are absolute, so learning to operate within them is requisite to living in harmony, fulfilling your purpose, and recreating Eden.

Knowing how *you*, as an integral part of this grand and perfect design, fit into the universal scheme of things will help you do what is needed to effectively play your part in it. Playing your part in the Whole of Creation is essential to your happiness—indeed, it is essential in recreating Eden and dwelling in harmony. As you will soon see, your primary role is extremely simple, yet immensely powerful and absolutely vital.

While you read this chapter, it will be helpful to keep an open mind (one of your most valuable evolutionary qualities) and suspend any preconceived ideas you may have. You can always reclaim them later if you want to! The following explanation may be vastly different than any you have considered before, or it may be somewhat familiar to you, but the concepts brought forth in this chapter are pivotal. Even if the information seems at first to be "old hat" to you, I believe you will find it expressed just differently enough to cause you to shift or expand your perception and see things in a new and helpful way.

By internalizing the information herein, you will gain the combination to open the Garden Gate!

OUR UNIVERSE IS ONE ENORMOUS, UNIFIED *WHOLE*, and every single component of it is vital to its integrity and function. There is nothing superfluous—everything and *everyone* in it has a purpose, including you, of course. It is intricately designed so that each particle, each being plays a very specific part that is vital to its overall success. In turn, each being's success depends on how accurately it fulfills its intended function. In other words, your personal success—your capacity for inner satisfaction and true fulfillment—is dependent upon how accurately you align with and fulfill *your* intended function within the Whole.

The Great Intelligence—Source—that initiates this massive creation exists at the very core of it, as well as all throughout it, with every part of Creation being the manifestation of its thought patterns. We are all linked with this Loving Intelligence, and we are all fueled by the emanation of it. This emanation is Life Force Energy, also known as *Love*.

Your very survival, as well as your success in playing the role you came to Earth to play, depends upon your circulation of Life Force Energy, as Life Force is what keeps the part of Creation that is you, vital. In other words, being connected with Source and engaged with the flow of Life Force is what makes you alive. If you become disengaged from the flow of Life Force, you, or at least the *physical manifestation* of you, are dead!

Sadly, most of us live in a state somewhere in between total aliveness and death, receiving and circulating less and less Life Force as the years pass, operating with a growing deficit of the energy required to be fully alive. This increasing shortage of Life Force causes degeneration and decline, and is the cause of illness and aging. When your physical body, through aging or through trauma, can no longer amply receive and circulate Life Force Energy, it dies and goes into a disintegration process so that its matter can be broken down into a simple state and converted into usable energy again. Though forms die and change, Life Force never dies—it is simply transformed and utilized for another purpose.

So, the most important survival task for any living, embodied entity such as you is the maintaining of its circulation of Life Force Energy. There is only one way you can do that, and that is to be properly positioned in the Divine Design and thus aligned with the Source of Life Force, utilizing the tools built into you for keeping Life Force flowing freely. Essentially, that's pretty much all you need to do to recreate Paradise as well. That—and doing what you were put here to do—which some (namely me) might postulate is one and the same.

Sounds pretty simple, doesn't it? And it is. Then again, it has proven to be harder than it sounds. After all, as I explained in the preceding chapter, most of humanity has forgotten these things, so current conditions on Earth are not supportive of staying correctly aligned to receive ample Life Force from Source, nor are they supportive of maintaining the effective use of your built-in tools for keeping this Life Force circulating effectively. In fact, conditions on Planet Earth have not been at all conducive to survival, much less to thriving. Indeed, your deterioration started about as soon as you popped out of the womb. That old saw that goes "As soon as you're born, you begin to die" is sad but true—at least that's the way it has been on Earth for a long, long time.

As a human being and integral part of the Whole of Creation, you are designed to perform a unique set of functions. Actually, "you"—the truth of you—is not the personality or ego-self you may be used to considering as you. You are far more than that. You are a manifestation of a specific idea of the Creator, designed to experience and enjoy existence in human form for a time while fulfilling your purpose here. In other words, you, as an *aspect* of the Creator, provide the Creator with the capacity to function as a specialized type of human on Earth. Your unique makeup, particular abilities, interests, strengths, and, yes, even "weaknesses" make you the one and only one who can be you! *Without you, this particular manifestation of the Creator would not exist.* Regardless of any outward accomplishments you may or may not have achieved, this one fact means that you truly *are* a V.I.P.!

Have you ever wished to be somebody else? I certainly have. Years ago, when I was in a class designed to accelerate spiritual growth, a young woman, a guest of the instructor, took the podium and pretty much blew the room away. I do not recall her name but for the sake of the story, we'll call her "Serena Johnson."

She was beautiful and strong and articulate. She stood tall, regal, and self-assured, looking like a Nubian princess in a business suit. Her aura of great substance and radiance telegraphed a spiritual maturity and confidence that I had never before encountered— and immediately coveted. As she spoke, her clarity and power were like beacons cutting through a fog to illuminate our consciousness, and I was overcome with envy. I wanted to be like her. Or more accurately, I wanted to *be* her! I wanted to have what she had, know what she knew, and do what she did. "Oh, God," I implored. "Why can't I be Serena Johnson?"

The answer came immediately and forcefully, leaving no room for argument. "Because I already have a perfectly good Serena Johnson. I don't need another one. What I need is YOU and what only *you* can provide."

And so it is with you as well. Despite what you think about yourself, what God needs is the unique amalgam of characteristics that is *you*. Regardless of what most of us feel in adolescence, where the tendency is to believe that being like everyone else is the key to survival, *diversity* is the real name of the game here on Planet Earth; that is so the Creator can experience every possibility of Himself.[1] There is no mistake whatever that every human being is unique. Just as each fingerprint and each snowflake that is created is different from any other, so too is every living being. You are one of a kind, and without *you*, a facet of God is unexpressed.

Yes, every human has her or his own particular, one-of-a-kind role to play. But there is one role that precedes all others. It is the role that *every human* is designed to play because it is so crucial in the Creator's design. Aside from the particular details of your individual assignment on Planet Earth (the job you are designed to do based on your own particular interests and abilities), *your* primary *purpose as a human being is to be a receiver, carrier, and transmitter of Life Force Energy, also known as "Love."*

Radiating Love is the most important task you can fulfill as a human being. The more freely and capably you receive, circulate, and transmit the Love that is being constantly emanated by Source, the more vital you are in the scheme of things. And because this is what you are designed to do, *doing it naturally positions you for the optimal flow of Life Force.* Indeed, as a perk, doing your job as a transmitter of Love makes you healthy and happy and raises you up within reach of the Garden Gate! The Divine Design is chockfull of such magnificent reciprocations. There are unending benefits that are automatically ours for doing and being that which we were designed to do and be. Talk about the rewards of success!

When you are primarily radiating Love, you are succeeding where it counts the most, despite anything else you may accomplish on this Earth. It is that simple. *When we increase the sum total of Love on Earth, we are successes in doing our primary job as humans.* As long as you are being a transmitter of Love, anything else you

---

1 God is not simply male nor simply female, but a perfect balance of both. For lack of a better term, I'm using the male pronoun for now because of the nature of God's polarity as it relates to us, which you will understand as the chapter proceeds.

achieve as a human being is gravy.

There are additional benefits for performing the task of being a transmitter of Love. The only way you can be optimally effective at it is to fully circulate Life Force/Love throughout your body-mind, and that just happens to be the requirement for optimal health and true happiness. Doing your job as a transmitter of Love brings you joy and radiant health! If knowledge of your *individual* role is what you crave, you'll be happy to know that doing your job as a transmitter of Love means that you are automatically hooked up to the Great Intelligence that holds the knowledge of what your other individual, divinely ordained roles and purposes are and how to go about fulfilling them! Not only that, you are in position to receive all the energy you need to carry them out. Neat design, eh?

IT IS TRULY IMPOSSIBLE TO FULLY DESCRIBE A MULTIDIMENSIONAL CREATION of infinite systems within systems—where energy is continually being projected out and taken in all at the same time, where reality is more closely described as holographic than linear. I am going to attempt, however, to create a very simple picture for you that will give you a basic and utilitarian sense of how Life Force Energy relates with Itself and how you are designed to relate with It.

Everything in the Universe is simply energy moving—and though physicists are still arguing about the exact nature of this movement, we'll call it *vibration* until a more accurate and useful term comes along. For now, we'll say that everything is simply energy vibrating at a particular *frequency*. The vibrational rate of energy determines how it manifests. For example, the highest frequency energy our senses can detect is light, the slowest is dense matter, and vibrating at a rate somewhere in between is sound. But there is a much broader spectrum of energy; we simply cannot register all of it with the five senses we routinely use—at least not while we're at the lower vibrational levels most humans are currently operating. This is where our imaginations come in.

Envision the energy with the highest vibrational rate or frequency as being at the Core of Creation—the ultimate concentration of Life Force/Love, and the slowest as being farthest away from the Core, with the lowest concentration of Life Force/Love. Imagine that Creation is configured like a sun,[2] with the greatest energy in the center and rays of energy extending outward, decreasing in concentration and frequency the farther away from the Core they get.

Along those rays exist every type of entity in its own specific band or range of frequency relative to the Core of Creation. Everything, everyone, and every condition exists within a particular range of frequency and cannot exist outside that range. Each has its own place in the spectrum of Life Force Energy and, depending on that designated place, may manifest closer to or farther from the Core of Creation. And the way the whole thing is designed, you, or any other entity, can only *directly* connect with the energy vibrating at the level just above, adjacent to, or just below the level of your own range of vibration.

For example, you in your physical body, vibrating at the rate that you do, cannot directly connect with the Core—the vibrational intensity there would "fry" your body and energy circuits and cause them to be annihilated, just as getting too close to the sun would. As a human, your specified place in the design is at a lower vibrational level—which is *not* to be confused with an *inferior* vibrational level—and that is where you are designed to be. (Chapter 4 is devoted to exactly how you are meant to connect with higher vibratory levels adjacent to the Core of Creation.)

So you can't connect directly to the Core, and by the same token, you (your consciousness, that is) cannot fully interface with the slower vibrations of the physical world—at least not without the mediation of your *body*. On Planet Earth, only those privileged with a body, or "Earth suit," can fully participate in the unique physical experiences available here or, more importantly, perform the vital human function of infusing Love into the physical world.

---

2 While science is coming to understand Creation as being configured more like a bagel than an orb, we are going to use creative license here to try and understand an aspect of how energy relates with itself in the simplest way possible.

25

A living, embodied being such as you are is the product of the merging of higher vibrational energy of pure Spirit and the lower vibrational energy of materiality. By marrying these two levels of vibration, your body provides Spirit with a necessary energy interface with the physical world. Because your primary mission as a human is to provide a conduit for higher vibrational energy—Love—to merge with the physical realm on this planet, *your body is the equipment that allows you to do your job here on Earth.* You are the nexus between two levels of being.

As a human, this is your particular place in the Divine Design—the place that, when you occupy it, keeps you in the optimal position relative to the Core of Creation, the Source of Life Force Energy, for optimal energy and an optimal experience of life. There is, however, something standing in the way of this optimal alignment. There is a part of you that prevents you from achieving and sustaining the correct positioning for the job you were designed to do, and it is the thing that has to be changed. We will soon be getting to just what that is.

TO SUM UP WHAT WE'VE LOOKED AT SO FAR, your proximity to the Core of Creation determines your frequency, and your vibrational frequency determines how close you are to the Core of Creation. When you are operating at your optimal frequency, you are as close to Source/the Core of Creation as is possible for you to be as a human. Doing your job as a conduit of Love keeps you as close to the Source of Life Force as is possible, keeps your frequency up, keeps your body healthy, and is a requirement for living in the state of being we call Paradise. And the converse is true: the only way you can do your job as a perfect conduit of Love is to position yourself as close to Source as is possible for a human, thus keeping your frequency up.

Now here's one of the most powerful realizations I have ever had—so utterly simple and, in retrospect, so obvious. It is what this book and the whole "Paradise Process" are built upon: *The Garden of Eden is a positioning relative to Source, the Core of Creation. It is a frequency.* It is the maximum frequency at which a human being can manifest. It is the frequency at which you and I were *designed to thrive,* and, when we are operating at that frequency, we are back in the Garden!

It's just that simple.

YES, THE UNIVERSE IS TOTALLY MADE UP OF ENERGY RELATING WITH ENERGY. And, there is a facet of the way it is designed to relate that we need to grasp. The principle upon which the Whole of Creation operates is what we will call "Prime Principle." At its foundation is something so exquisitely simple, we studied it in elementary school science class. This most primary of principles is based on the union of opposites. Remember? Opposites attract. Your teacher likely demonstrated this with magnets.

This law that governs how magnets interact with each other also holds true throughout all Creation and governs every facet of it from the minutest operation to the grandest. Everything, from the formation of an atom to the blooming of a rose in your garden, from the movement of galaxies to the way the freeway flows—or doesn't—is under the jurisdiction of Prime Principle. This includes every facet of your life. So to better understand it, we'll go back to that science class of your childhood.

In this early lesson on magnetic force, you learned that magnets have two sides with different polarities. You learned that one side of the magnet was positive, and the other was negative. You learned that if you tried to put two magnets together with the same polarity sides facing, they would push away from each other. And, that if you flipped one of the magnets around so that the side with opposite polarity was facing the other, they would pull toward each other with a magical force and lock together as if they were glued.

Did your science teacher tell you that she was teaching you about the one great natural law that governs all that exists in our universe? Did she tell you that what she was teaching you about magnets held the map for getting back to Eden? Not likely. But she was—and she probably didn't even know it!

Before we go further, we need to get a couple of things straight. Let's look at the words "positive" and "negative." These words are popularly used today to mean "good" and "bad"—terms that infer *judgment*. In chapter 3, you will come to understand the folly of judgment in general, but for now, let it suffice to say that in this discussion, we will use "positive" and "negative" to denote *polarity* only.

Likewise, let's clarify something about the use of two other popularly utilized terms—"masculine" and "feminine." We normally associate these terms with "men" and "women" respectively. And they are certainly sex-related terms—but in this discourse and throughout this book, they are not intended to be *gender*-related, rather they will be utilized to describe polarity and will be used interchangeably with the terms "positive" and "negative."

These, too, have *nothing* to do with judgment. Equating the term "feminine" with the term "negative" is *not* a judgment. It does not imply in any way that "feminine" is bad. It merely describes its *polarity*. Likewise, equating the term "positive" with "masculine" does not mean "masculine" is "good" or somehow better than "feminine." It, too, describes its *polarity only*.

With that out of the way, let's do some experimenting with magnets. Unless you happen to have a set of unidirectional disc or ring-type magnets on hand, you will need to use your imagination for this part. If it's a bit of a challenge to follow this without having the actual magnets in hand, please just relax and hang in there with it as best you can. It will reward you with some insights that are transformational!

Let's say you have a dozen little magnets, and they are marked as to polarity. Each magnet has both a masculine and a feminine side. The positive or masculine side is marked with a " + " (plus sign), and the negative or feminine side is marked with a "-" (minus sign).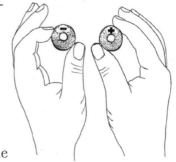

Pick one magnet up and hold it so its "masculine" side is facing out. The characteristic of its masculine side is to project or *radiate* energy. Now pick up another magnet in your other hand and be sure its "feminine" side is facing toward the masculine side of the first magnet. The characteristic demonstrated by the feminine side is to accept or *receive* energy.

Now bring the two magnets together just close enough so that you can feel a pulling sensation. The force that is created by the interaction of the masculine magnet with the feminine magnet is called *attraction*. Now bring the magnets closer and allow them to come together. When you do this, what happens is called *union*.

The unified magnets have, in essence, become one, but the power that they now exert together is stronger than the power they exerted individually. This power is called *unified radiance*. You will see that there is still one masculine side and one feminine side visible. And each polarity is demonstrating its respective characteristic. The side marked "masculine" is *projecting* energy. The side marked "feminine" is *receiving* energy. For all intents and purposes, unless you exert effort to pry them apart, they stay together and now possess the qualities of one larger magnet with a greater capacity to radiate and attract.

Next, hold your newly created, more powerful *unified* magnet in one hand, with the masculine side facing out. In the other hand hold another single magnet with the feminine side facing the unified magnet. Bring them close enough together to feel the pull. This time the pull feels uneven. This time the greater power of the unified magnet more easily pulls the other magnet to it. If you do this again adding yet another magnet, you will feel that the power of the three magnets stuck together is much greater than just the two unified magnets and so on.

Now I will ask you to really stretch your capacity to imagine! Pretend that the Core of Creation is one whale of a strong magnet—actually, the *ultimate* unified magnet, made up of all the smaller magnets in existence (which would be everything in existence—*everything* is a magnet of sorts). Imagine that coming from this great unified magnet is immense unified radiance. (Remember that the terms *radiating, radiation,* and *radiance* refer to the masculine characteristic of projecting outward, but in order for it to be possible, both masculine and feminine forces must come together and unify.) Imagine that the "out-facing sides" of this grand magnet are marked with a "+" and are, as are all things in unified radiance mode, demonstrating the masculine characteristic of *projecting* energy.

Now think back to what happens if you try to put two magnet sides with the same polarity together. They repel, and it is impossible for them to make a connection. With that in mind, if you are a magnet and you want to be unified with that grand magnet called Source which is projecting or radiating energy—a masculine action—then what quality or polarity will bring you into union with it? That's right. Your feminine or *receptive* side will. (What your feminine/receptive aspect is will be clarified soon, but in the meantime, please understand that you have one, no matter your gender.)

So if you want to be unified with Source—and you definitely do—you must have the feminine aspect of your being facing or available to Source. In other words, your receptivity must be to the radiation of Source, *not* to the other "magnets" out there. Why? Because when your receptive or feminine side is to other magnets, it means that your masculine, projecting side is to Source. Because Source is *radiating* energy (masculine mode), if you are presenting the *same* polarity to Source, by universal law, the Prime Principle, *you are automatically repelled.* When you are repelled from Source, it creates a magnetic gap in the frequency hierarchy, separating you from Source, pushing you down in frequency, farther from Source and farther from Eden.

However, *when your receptivity* (feminine side) *is turned to Source* as it is designed to be, *you are automatically unified with Source,* and your energy acts as part of the unified radiance of Source, channeling Source's immense Love to the world. (Remember, that's your job.) When this alignment occurs, your masculine, radiating side is facing outward to those other magnets, and not only do you channel a powerful stream of Love in and through you and out to the world, but the only magnets that can join with you are other magnets that are receptive—receptive to Source—and, thus, in harmony. Any magnets that are *out* of alignment with Source, and thus *out* of harmony, are automatically repelled and *cannot connect with you,* ensuring that your experience is one of ease and harmony, maintaining your frequency at the level where Eden manifests.

By the same token, when your receptivity is *not* to Source and is instead turned to other magnets, you are *repelled* from union with Source. To compound the problem, when your receptivity is to those other magnets and not to Source, you are also magnetic to and aligned with other energies that are repelled from Source. Just as you might imagine, these energies are *not* loving and harmonious. When you are aligned with them, your experience is not one of ease and harmony, and your frequency drops in proportion to your alignment with them.

We will call this state *reverse polarity.* Reverse polarity, particularly in the extreme, is what is commonly referred to as "evil"—but if we are to regain Eden, we will need to let go of the concepts of "good" and "evil." (In chapter 3, you will see why.) The important thing to remember is that when you are in reverse polarity, you are repelled from Source. When you are repelled from Source, you are pulled down in frequency and thus are out of the range of frequency where Paradise manifests. Not only that, everything below you in the frequency hierarchy is affected by this magnetic gap as well. Which explains why the world is in the mess it's in—not just because of you, personally, but because of all the humans who are sustaining the magnetic gap and keeping all under their jurisdiction from perfect alignment with Source.

Based on Prime Principle, then, you attract energy (events, circumstances, things) according to your focus and receptivity. This is where the *seemingly* opposite concept to the Prime Principle, that of "like attracts like," comes in. In actuality, "like attracts like" is simply an integral facet of Prime Principle, since by virtue of what you are receptive to, and thus, what you are radiating out, you attract other magnets that are focused in the same direction.

Though this illustration is focused on the *radiance* of Source— the masculine aspect that is pushing energy outward from the Core, and our correct relationship to it—Source also has an *equally powerful feminine aspect* pulling energy inward back to the Core to complete the cycle that initiates there. And the same principle applies as it relates to the magnet we're calling "you": When you are in alignment, your masculine aspect is pointed toward the feminine, receptive pole of the unified magnets we're calling "God." To understand how this can be, imagine Creation as a circular bank of unified magnets, where all the arrows of energy movement are pointing in the same direction. There is radiation *out from* the Core, and at the same time, there is a receiving *into* the Core.

So, when you are focused on and receptive to Source, you are properly aligned to be radiating the love from Source, and as a result, to send it back to Source in sequence. In this state, you attract other magnets that are properly aligned, maintaining your optimal frequency and proper position in the energy hierarchy for a harmonious experience. When your receptivity is to anything other than Source, you attract other magnets that are out of alignment, repelled from Source, and lower in frequency. And that connects you with energy in reverse polarity, which pulls you down in frequency and out of Eden. Obviously, then, the trick to residing in Eden is to maintain a constant receptivity to Source. Naturally, how to do that is covered in upcoming chapters.

NOW THAT I HAVE SHOWN YOU THE BASICS OF PRIME PRINCIPLE, I need to explain that things aren't exactly as simple as, "Some things are aligned with Source and some things are not." If you were to completely lose your alignment with Source, you could not sustain the amount of Life Force needed to operate your body and your body would die (something that, for millennia, has happened to every human sooner or later as a consequence of their imperfect alignment and resulting reduction in Life Force).

Fortunately, much of each human is *involuntarily* aligned with Source and perfectly receptive because human consciousness—free will—is not directly involved in its operation. Think, for example, of the autonomic nervous system that controls a multitude of physical processes in your body. It works whether you think about it or not, and, unless you are an advanced yogi, you probably have little or no conscious control over these processes—the autonomic nervous system keeps them in alignment. But the operations that your conscious mind controls are what are in danger of being pulled out of alignment and can ultimately affect even those systems ruled by the autonomic nervous system. How your conscious mind participates in your exile from Eden and how it can participate in your restoration to it will be covered very soon. It is, actually, the crux of the matter.

For now, let's just acknowledge that most everything and everyone is an amalgam of energies both aligned with Source and out of alignment. In ordinary terms, it's safe to say that no one and no thing is "all bad" or "all good." (You will soon see, though, why even using the terms "bad" and "good" is folly.) At this point in the story of humanity, every human and human-created or human-influenced event, circumstance, or thing is a mixture of both energy in alignment and energy in reverse polarity. And sometimes those magnets are flipping back and forth so fast it is dizzying!

Bringing more and more of these magnets in reverse polarity into alignment is the process we will be undertaking. As we do this, we will rise higher and higher in frequency until we close the magnetic gap completely, experience the perfect alignment with Source we were designed to have, channel immense Love through us, and reach the level where Eden manifests. By virtue of this, all the elements below us in the energy hierarchy will spontaneously come back into alignment as well, restoring Earth to the glory she is designed to embody. The Prime Principle and the power of unified radiance assure that this will be a whole lot easier than it may sound.

In fact, struggling and working to achieve this is completely antithetical to the process of restoration! Despite the disruption in it at the human level, the Creator's design for harmony is firmly in place, of total integrity, and radiating immense power. What is required to align with it is not to *do* anything so much as it is to *allow* its immense magnetic power to draw us back into our proper place. There is a part of you, though, that is actually working hard—very hard—to keep you out of alignment! We will be addressing this aspect of you and how to convince it to let go and go with the flow, so to speak, in an upcoming chapter.

Returning to Eden, then, is a simple matter of regaining your proper alignment with the Divine Design and thus with Source, a.k.a. "God." You do this by being fully receptive and obedient to God instead of anything lower, and allowing yourself to be realigned by the magnetic force of the Divine Design. Once you achieve that, you're pretty much home free, with your life an experience of perfect ease and unimaginable bliss! If it's so easy, you may say, and if the frequency of Eden is where we originated and were designed to live, what happened? Why in heaven's name did humanity leave in the first place? For that answer, we will need to go back a ways— back to the biblical Garden of Eden.

CHAPTER THREE

Losing Eden:
The First Humans Choose
Misalignment

*T*O EXPLAIN HOW HUMANITY FIRST CAUSED THE "MAGNETIC GAP" between itself and the very Source of Life Force Energy, dooming itself to exile from the harmonious, blissful state we're calling "the Garden," and how that state of separation is perpetuated day after day, generation after generation, I am going to interpret for you the story of "The Fall of Man," which is found in Genesis, the first book of the Old Testament of the *Holy Bible*. There are countless interpretations of this story that offer valuable insights into the human condition, but, in my opinion, none are more relevant to our history and to our destiny than the one I'm going to share with you.

In this interpretation, Adam and Eve portray the first man and first woman. They not only symbolize humanity, but also represent the two primary aspects of the human mind—the masculine and the feminine, the conscious mind and the subconscious mind.

(I am referring to *any* human mind whether in a male-gendered or a female-gendered human being.) The story itself shows how these two aspects of the mind came to operate in a way that caused humans to lose their home in Paradise and begin losing Life Force, leading, of course, to deterioration and death, not to mention, an inharmonious and stressful life experience.

The cast of characters for our story includes:

- *God,* representing the Creator, the Source of Life Force, the Perfect Provider, the ultimate unified magnet demonstrating ultimate Unified Radiance.

- The *Garden of Eden,* symbolizing the experience of perfect magnetic alignment, of total Oneness with God, and the complete harmony and ease inherent in that state of being.

- *God's voice,* representing the guiding voice of Spirit sounding within every human.

- *Adam and Eve,* representing the first humans as well as the two primary aspects of the human mind.

- *Eve,* representing the inner feminine, the receptive pole of the human magnet; the aspect of the human mind that is designed to be perfectly receptive to Spirit, thus flawlessly interfaced to receive Life Force from Source, and guidance as to how to utilize this Life Force.

- *Adam,* representing the inner masculine, the projecting, radiating pole of the human magnet; the conscious, objective aspect of the human mind that is designed to use the Life Force and guidance that Eve receives from Source to interact with the world according to Spirit's instructions.

- The *serpent,* representing the lower aspect of the human mind that exists by virtue of reverse polarity energy (indeed, it cannot exist without it), using seduction to manipulate Eve and Adam into activating the subschema for disharmony to meet its survival needs.

- The *Tree of Life*, representing Oneness, the matrix for harmony and wholeness and the original schema of the Divine Design.

- The *Tree of the Knowledge of Good and Evil*, representing duality, the matrix for disharmony and deterioration, and the subschema of the Divine Design.

- The *fruit of the Tree of the Knowledge of Good and Evil*, representing the forbidden *concepts* of duality, of opposites.

- The *eating of the fruit*, symbolizing the choosing of the serpent's agenda over obeying God; the action that sets in motion humanity's exile from the unified state we call "Paradise."

As you may recall from reading the Book of Genesis, it states that God created form out of the void and found it pleasing. It says that once God had manifested His perfect design, He needed someone to represent Him and take care of His interests in the beautiful world He had made. So He decided to create humans as stewards and co-creators.

These beings were sort of mini-versions of God "Himself,"[1] which He placed on Earth to care for it. Thus, the first humans were made in God's "image and likeness," with the power to create in the same way that God did. Because God had unlimited creative power, God gave humans free will, also, so that their creations would be unlimited as well. Inherent in this free will and unlimited creative power was the power to choose—to choose whether or not to be obedient to Him. This gift of free will certainly set up a dynamic that ensured excitement in Creation! You might ask, "Why in the world would God take the chance of giving humans free will?" We will come to that shortly.

---

1 As we know from our imaginary magnet experiments, God, the Source, is equally masculine and feminine, but in relationship to Adam and Eve in this story, God represented the action of the Unified Radiance phase, the impulse or radiation of God which is masculine, thus, it is accurate to call God "Him" in this context.

According to the story, Adam and Eve were the original inhabitants of Earth, residing in what we now call Paradise, or "The Garden of Eden." God entrusted them with complete access to, and dominion over, all the wonders of Eden except for one particular tree, which he told them was reserved for Him alone.

These first Earth-humans enjoyed a stress-free life of total bliss, partaking of God's bounteous gifts, lacking nothing. They lived in a state of perfection, of total energy alignment and flow, at the highest possible frequency a human can exist. They were in complete oneness with all Creation, relying on God for everything. Their only job was to tend the garden by radiating Love to it, thus creating beauty and harmony while enjoying the splendors of their perfect world.

The creations of these stewards of Eden were all perfect and harmonious because the ideas that provided the blueprints for them came to them straight from the omnipotent, omniscient Mind of God. Everything they thought and did was divine in origin because of their perfect alignment with Source; everything they touched was blessed by the pure Love they radiated. Beauty such that we can only imagine was the atmosphere they maintained, with balance and harmony being the natural order of things in their world. All was right in the Garden.

That is, all was right until the day Adam and Eve made a notorious decision with considerable ramifications. On this day, they disobeyed God and did the one thing that He had commanded them not to do. They "ate of the fruit of the Tree of the *Knowledge* of Good and Evil." That, the Creator had told them, was the one and only tree that was reserved for Him and Him alone, and if they ate of its fruit, they would surely die. That warning was good enough for the first woman and first man and they left it alone—for a while, anyway.

Then along came a serpent who, in this interpretation, represents the lower-frequency aspect of the human mind that cannot exist without energy in reverse polarity. (Some Bible versions go so far as to call this serpent "Satan." We'll just call it the "embodiment of energy in reverse polarity.") Because the serpent represents the lowest-frequency part of humans, it seems appropriate that its physical form, relative to a human's, is low—crawling-on-the-ground low.

The serpent symbol relates to the reptilian brain, the primitive part of the human brain that, among other things, houses our lower urges and is primarily concerned with survival issues. It is where *fear* originates. The reptilian brain, when in balance with the other parts of the brain, is not "evil" and, in fact, is what controls your autonomic brain, lung and heart functions, etc. It only becomes a problem when certain aspects of it are out of control.

Genesis describes this serpent as being the subtlest of all God's creatures—in other words, it was low key, insidious, and hard to identify as untrustworthy—just as energy in reverse polarity is often hard to identify as dangerous to humans. It was *so* subtle, it was hiding out inside of them! The serpent's plan was to manipulate Adam and Eve into activating the subschema of the Divine Design, the "flip side" of the Divine Design for Wholeness and Harmony, so that it could be fed by reverse-polarity energy.

In the story, the serpent began smooth-talking Eve, the *feminine* aspect of the Adam and Eve duo, baiting her by asking, "Did God really say you must not eat from any tree in the Garden?"

Eve replied, "He said we can partake of any of the trees in the Garden *except* the one in the midst of it— the Tree of the Knowledge of Good and Evil. We are to eat freely of the crown jewel of the Garden, the Tree of Life, but we are not to so much as touch the Tree of the Knowledge of Good and Evil. He said if we do, we will surely die."

The serpent was ready with its argument. "Nah—you won't die," it said. "God just told you that because he doesn't want you to eat it and become all-wise! He knows when you do, your *eyes will be opened* and you will be as powerful as he is. What could be wrong with that? Wouldn't you like to be as powerful and as wise as God? Go ahead—it is succulent and juicy and you know you want it. Come on—eat it!"

The sales job was effective. Eve looked at the forbidden fruit and saw that it was attractive and promised to be delicious. That, coupled with the prospect of ultimate power and wisdom, was just too, too tempting, so she took a bite and then offered one to Adam.

Adam knew it was wrong but he couldn't resist either—he was programmed to do as Eve directed him to do—and so he ate the forbidden fruit, too. With that, their "eyes were opened," they saw that they were naked (individual, separate) and they were doomed.

THAT WAS SOME POTENT FRUIT, EH? What did eating it represent? Eating the forbidden fruit, the Bible story says, "opened their eyes." What is the significance of this wording? Having their "eyes opened" is a metaphor for having a new *perception.* Having their "eyes opened" means that they were seeing something for the first time. What was it God had not wanted them to see? What was it He had warned them to stay away from? It was a concept. This concept is called *duality.* The fruit of the Tree of the Knowledge of Good and Evil is the perception of duality. What is duality? The dictionary defines duality as the view that the universe is under the dominion of two opposing principles—one of which is *good* and the other *evil.*

What was so deadly about this? Within the term "duality" is the idea of *"more than one."* This constituted a revolution in these first humans' perceptions because in their consciousness up to then, there had only been *one* unified being that included everything, and only *one* principle—harmony—the principle they were designed to operate from. There had never existed a concept of *separateness* or of two opposing principles, *good* and *evil,* (or in terms that are more truly descriptive, *harmony* and *disharmony*). You could say that in the Garden, all was One and It was all good—you *could* say that but, of course, without the concept of "evil," there *is* no concept of "good."

The Divine Design is, first and foremost, a schema for Oneness, Wholeness, and Harmony. Inherent in it, however, is its *opposite*— a subschema for separateness, duality, and disharmony. This subschema is the *reverse* of the Creator's design for Wholeness— not evil (at least not without human thought energy), simply opposite. The problem with the duality schema as it relates to us is that *we were designed to thrive in the schema for harmony.* For humans, the schema for separateness and disharmony is deadly. God had warned Adam and Eve to stay away from duality because He knew that it would activate the schema for disharmony. And it did.

As long as the first humans had been completely immersed in Oneness, reverse polarity could not affect them. Because the concept of opposites is nonexistent in the state of Oneness, the schema for reverse polarity had never before been activated in human experience. The only way it could be activated was through duality thinking. It only exists as a dynamic in the human world when humans activate and feed it with their thoughts. This is what those first humans did by eating the fruit of the Tree of the Knowledge of Good and Evil.

Suddenly, they were no longer fully immersed in the totally harmonious state of Oneness but were viewing their world in terms of "self" and "other." Now they were experiencing things from the standpoint of *observer* for the first time, something not possible in the state of Oneness. They were seeing their world, as well as perceiving God for the first time, in terms of something *external* to themselves. They saw themselves as separate from God, from the Garden, from each other—*and thus,* at least in their reality and experience thereof, *they were.* And the reverse-polarity world had a foothold.

The immense significance of this new development cannot be overstated.

LET'S LOOK AT THE STORY OF THE FALL IN TERMS OF MAGNETS AND POLARITY. Initially, there was seamless alignment of all the "magnets" of Creation. Everything was perfectly aligned and operating in right sequence so that harmony reigned and Life Force was flowing uninterrupted throughout. As long as Eve, the feminine, receptive pole of the unified "human magnet" was in correct position and completely available to receive energy and instruction from God (who was, if you'll recall our magnet illustration, radiating in *masculine* polarity), and as long as Adam, the masculine pole of the unified human magnet, was in perfect union with Eve and able to take these instructions and act upon them, and radiate the Love onward toward the receptive aspect of the Heart of God, there was perfect union and all was well in Paradise.

But—and this is critical—once Eve's receptivity became available to the serpent, a reverse-polarity entity aligned with the schema for disharmony, the human magnet was flipped around and *repelled* from Source, causing them to no longer be aligned for their customary complete flow of Life Force Energy and divine information. Thus a sacred union was broken, enabling the perception of being separate. This was the advent of the deadly magnetic gap that still exists between Source and humanity.

The Bible says that after the fruit incident, God "put enmity between Eve and the serpent." So now she had a distaste for the entities of reverse polarity. Adam, however, identified with this new world of separateness and found that he was at home there, even though it was a harder existence. From his new position facing the gap, his viewpoint was that of separation from Source. Without the experience of his direct connection with Source, he even began to think of *himself* as God in this new state of being. This was the birth of the human ego, the part of the human mind that is invested in individuation, in separateness, that sees no alternative.

With Eve wanting nothing to do with this alien world and its manifestations, and Adam enjoying it so much, a power struggle ensued—a power struggle that lasts until this day. Before sending them out of Eden, God pronounced that as part of their punishment, Adam would, henceforth, rule over Eve. So no matter how much she wanted to return to their original state, as the flip side of the human magnet, she couldn't do so as long as Adam wanted to continue to align with the world of the serpent and stay separate. So Eve did the best she could and aligned them with Source whenever Adam was asleep or otherwise not paying attention.

Because of this relationship breakdown, Adam operated more and more from input through the senses gathered from the largely misaligned world, and from the concepts he could construct on his own without the benefit of God's wisdom. He used these as his guidance system in lieu of divine guidance via Eve. Remember, Adam's rightful job is to use the instructions and energy coming through Eve to do Spirit's bidding in the world, but now that he was polarized into the world of separation, he lost touch with the understanding of his divinely ordained role, and lacking a sense of authentic purpose, Adam developed his own agendas—fear-based agendas that are aligned with the serpent's agendas of dominance, territoriality, hoarding, mating, and other survival issues.

Instead of interacting with the world on God's behalf as it was designed to do, the mind under the dominance of the masculine does so on its own behalf, based on a faulty idea of what is truly in its best interests. It operates in the world not to maintain harmony with the Whole, but to advance its own ideas of what is for its individual or tribal benefit. Because the masculine aspect of the mind sees separateness and fragmentation, it creates accordingly and for the purposes of maintaining that state. Without being aligned with Source via the inner feminine's perfect receptivity, it cannot see the whole picture, as it does not have the benefit of being hooked up to the omniscient wisdom of God. Yet it attempts to act as if it does.

What an inefficient, ineffective method that is! The current state of the world is evidence of the human mind's less-than-stellar ability to run things in harmony when operating without the total guidance of Spirit. There is no way that the masculine-dominated human mind, operating on its own, in alignment with the lowest-frequency part of us, can create the kind of harmony we yearn for and, indeed, were designed for. Until there is a reconciliation of the Adam and Eve within us, until the magnetic gap is closed by a restoration of the human mind to the way it was designed to operate, we will continue to experience a world out of harmony.

AS A RESULT OF THE GAP THAT NOW EXISTED between those first humans and Source, their frequency was lowered. It was lowered right out of Paradise! *Eden is a frequency.* Its "address" is at the top of the frequency hierarchy for human beings. When you drop below it in frequency, it does not exist in your experience. This high-frequency state of being is accessible only by being properly positioned relative to Source and completely unified with It for a full flow of Life

Force Energy. As soon as those first humans created a gap in their lifeline to Source, diminishing the flow of Life Force through them, they lowered their frequency below the range where Eden manifests and it was "Good-bye, Paradise." To them, Eden simply vanished, and they did not know how to get back to it. For the most part, humans have been absent from Eden ever since.

Yes, the fate of humanity was sealed by that first act of disobedience. The Bible story says that after the first humans had their eyes opened, God cursed them, exiling them from the Garden, condemning them to hard work, struggle, pain in childbirth, and most damning of all, Eve's subservience to Adam—and Adam's control over Eve. (Remember that, even though the Divine Design dictates that Adam follow Eve's lead, Adam now called the shots and insisted Eve support his separatist agenda.)

If ever there was a curse, this was surely one. Still, I am not sure it is entirely accurate to say that "God cursed them." I believe that God had simply established natural law from the beginning, and when they violated it, the punishment was built in. You see, all the difficulties Eve and Adam faced were only manifested because of the lower frequency they now inhabited—a frequency for which they were not designed. Such problems did not—and do not—exist at the higher levels of frequency in which human beings *are* designed to inhabit—the frequency of Eden.

Before the fruit incident, their oneness with all Creation had kept the first humans at optimal frequency, in total health and harmony, receiving a continuous flow of Life Force, lacking nothing. Once they lost their perfect alignment, however, they experienced the constant loss of Life Force that stemmed from not being hooked up correctly. Not only that, they had to deal with the harshness of living in the clashing currents of duality and the unrelenting stress caused by being out of harmony with the Whole, further serving to accelerate their deterioration.

There is only one fate for a being in a state of perpetual energy loss and deterioration. Violating God's preeminent law, Prime Principle, automatically brought not only the punishment of being locked out of the Garden and of enduring the life of hardship and suffering the *Bible* says God "cursed them" with, but it also condemned them to death. That law is still in place today, and the punishment for violating it is just the same as it was when the first humans did so. Yes, Adam and Eve were doomed to die because of their disobedience, and *so are we*. What may have seemed at first like a harmless indulgence in some delectable "fruit" had catapulted them into a treacherous world from which neither they—nor we— have yet to return.

WHEN THE FIRST HUMANS VIBRATIONALLY SEPARATED themselves from their Source by falling for the seduction of the serpent and disobeying God, they not only lost Life Force, they lost effortless access to all of God's vast, unlimited resources, including God's omniscience. This is quite ironic, being that what they were after in eating the forbidden fruit was *greater* wisdom! But the type of wisdom they sought was never even a possibility. They weren't, as we will examine more closely in a moment, designed to know "good" from "evil." And even more to the point, the crux of the matter wasn't that God didn't want them to be able to tell good from evil, the real issue was that He didn't want them to *perceive* things in terms of good and evil.

"Good and evil" was a *concept* that God did not want Adam and Eve to have. Remember, the forbidden fruit came *not* from the "Tree of Good and Evil" but from the "Tree of the *Knowledge* of Good and Evil." Though I am far from being a Hebrew scholar, I believe that the original Biblical writings could have possibly been translated as the "Tree of the *Concept* of Good and Evil."

Why is it important to make this seemingly subtle distinction? Because "good" and "evil" are notions—merely concepts—until humans empower them with their thought energy. They are not real things until they are given life by the highly creative human mind. Human beings are designed so that their thoughts are potent and have the capacity to create—this was a part of the Divine Design as, if you recall, God had made humans to be co-creators with Him. God knew that once the concept of good and evil became a part of their mental "software," they would create accordingly. Good and evil could not exist in our reality if we did not have them as "templates" in our minds. They could not exist if we did not empower them with our thought energy. The serpent would have no power if we did not give power to it.

Nor could the concept of good and evil continue to exist without a dynamic we call "judgment." For now that the concept existed, it had to be sustained by human minds making determinations about what was good and what was evil. The main problem with human judgment is that it requires us to think in terms of being separate from that which we're attempting to judge. Another is that we are simply not equipped to judge. To judge anything, you have to depend completely upon your own limited sensory abilities, being that you are necessarily disconnected from the ultimate wisdom of Great Spirit by virtue of the duality that is the precursor of judgment.

Because you, operating independently of Source, do not have the capacity to see and comprehend the whole picture, you can't possibly see enough to understand how the part you *can* see fits into the vast Wholeness, into the Divine Design. What might seem bad or wrong or inappropriate from your limited perspective may well be seen as purposeful and meaningful if you were able to grasp the whole gigantic picture the way the Greater Mind of God can. What may seem good may not be harmonious at all if seen from the highest perspective, and likewise, "bad" or "evil" may not be what you thought it was, either.

There is an old fable that illustrates this very well. It tells of a farmer whose horse runs away, leaving him no way to pull his plow. His neighbors say, "What bad luck!"

The farmer says, "Maybe so, maybe not."

Then, a week later, the horse returns, bringing several other wild horses with it, which the farmer can also train for work. The neighbors say, "What good luck!"

The farmer again says, "Maybe so, maybe not."

While trying to tame one of the wild horses, the farmer's son, whom the farmer depends on to help with the farm work, is thrown off and breaks a leg. "What awful luck!" everyone thinks.

The farmer says, "Maybe so, maybe not."

When, soon after, there is a call for all able-bodied young men to go to war, the farmer's son cannot go because of his injury. The neighbors see the broken leg as a blessing and exclaim, "What good luck!"

And again, the farmer says, "Maybe so, maybe not."

The farmer is wise to know that he doesn't have enough information to judge any of the events as good luck or bad. Humans do not have what it takes to be able to know everything necessary to make an accurate judgment. By virtue of your very design, even though you have been given remarkable abilities—*God's abilities*—as a "stand-alone human," you are simply not equipped to see the whole picture at once. You are not equipped to make an accurate determination of what is "good" and what is "evil."

Only when we are fully aligned with God do we have the complete picture—and the irony is, in that state, judgment is a nonexistent concept! At this stage of our evolution, until we are 100 percent realigned with Source, though we can have access to all of God's wisdom that we need in any given moment via correct alignment, we receive it on a "need-to-know" basis. We are, therefore, called upon to simply trust that God is in charge, despite how things may appear, and follow God's instructions step-by-step in the moment.

The only stance that puts us back in range of the Garden is to relate to events and indeed, to all of Creation, as the first humans did before they fell to the temptations of duality. Things were neither good nor evil—things simply *were*.

SINCE ADAM AND EVE LEFT THE GARDEN, the human mind has perpetuated the state of separation, of duality, of good and evil, and conditions on Planet Earth have become more and more misaligned down through the ages. Now the misaligned energy patterns here (think of a whole bunch of renegade magnets grouped together and repelled from Source) are so strongly established, with their unified radiance, they tend to affect whatever comes into their force fields.

Because *all* energy originates in and emanates from the Heart of God, these energies in reverse polarity are, in truth, Love, and can never *truly* be anything else. However, energy that has been influenced by the magnetic pull of the unified radiance of energies in reverse polarity can "forget" its true nature. Until the greater Unified Radiance of Love—energy aligned with Source—pulls it back into alignment with the schema for harmony, this "misguided" energy creates disharmony.

When energies in reverse polarity interface with energies aligned with Source, turbulence results. A sort of friction is created wherever these two opposing currents coexist, and the pull of the currents in opposite directions can tear the fabric of whatever comes under the magnetic influence of these forces in conflict. Because Earth is now a zone where both come together significantly—everything and everyone on Earth at this time is a mixture of harmony and disharmony—there is an immense amount of friction present here and, because of it, our experience of life is often harsh. And, because we as humans are an amalgamation of energies in both polarities, life in our own skins can be extremely uncomfortable and, sometimes, nearly unbearable. But there is a way to harmonize these energies and restore peace, both within and without.

Made in the "image and likeness" of the Heart of God, from which Love originates, the human heart is the instrument that is designed to not only receive Love and radiate it, but it is made to transform wayward energy back into its true nature. The human heart—not the physical organ, but the energy center located in the area of the heart called the heart chakra—has the capacity to take energy in reverse polarity and restore it to harmony instantly! First, of course, there must be proper alignment with Source. To transform energy in reverse polarity back into Love, our minds as well as our hearts must be "in the right place."

When we are aligned with Source and channeling enough Love through our hearts, we naturally cause energy in reverse polarity to "turn around" and become aware of itself as Love again! Like the powerful, unified magnet aligned with Source that we imagined in the last chapter, this awesome, high-vibrational energy has the power to flip the polarity of the misaligned energy and restore it to its original state—Love.

Because energies in reverse polarity are not aligned with Source, they are necessarily vibrating at a lower frequency. Energy vibrating at a *higher* frequency—that which is aligned with the very Source of all energy—is *always* stronger than energy at lower frequencies. It is a physical as well as a spiritual truth that higher-frequency energy pulls lower-frequency energy up to its level. Therefore, energy in reverse polarity can never be stronger than Love. *Love is the ultimate power.*

Just as the greater unified magnet has the power to pull other magnets into alignment, when enough human minds and hearts are properly aligned to fully receive and radiate the omnipotent Love from Source, *all* inharmonious energy will be restored to harmony. Then the cycle that began with Adam and Eve will be complete. That we are able to even comprehend this is an indicator that we are, at this time in history, closer than ever to resuming life in Paradise, our true home. As we undertake the process of realigning with Source, the power of our "realigned magnets" will pull more and more energy into alignment, and the results will be reflected in the increased state of harmony on Planet Earth and, of course, in our own lives.

AS STRANGE AS IT SEEMS, HUMANITY'S INITIAL "FALL FROM GRACE," its leave-taking from Paradise, and subsequent eons of misalignment may just have been a crucial part of the ongoing, larger creative process. Maybe Great Spirit, in order to complete a creative cycle, *chose* to experience the distortions of misalignment by purposely implanting the "fatal flaw" in humanity. Maybe the Creator wanted to experience every possibility of self-expression, both "light" and "dark," both high frequency and low. Perhaps the Creator wanted to see how long it would take before humanity figured out the security code to the Garden Gate. Or maybe it was an experiment the Creator devised to see just how misaligned and how far away from the core of Itself Its constituent parts could move before they were catapulted back to center. Maybe . . .

From our limited perspective, we simply cannot know. One thing is for sure though, if we deign to believe that we can discern whether the whole situation is "right" or "wrong," "good" or "evil," we are simply propelling ourselves out of alignment by presuming to make the judgment—not to mention that we are perpetuating the whole state of affairs. Only your ego—the part of you that maintains your illusions of duality, and thus the magnetic gap—needs to think it knows what's what, and needs to broadcast your judgments of such matters to others in an effort to gain status. This does not serve to elevate you in frequency! What *does* elevate you in frequency is to simply trust at all times and in all circumstances, that despite appearances, God is *always* in charge and always knows exactly what He is doing. Doubting that and disobeying God's ordinance is what initiated humanity's fall in frequency—its eviction from the Garden—to begin with!

Please don't take this to mean that if you observe something that seems to you to be out of harmony that you should do nothing, or that you should condone things that strike you as wrong. No, that is not what I am saying at all. What I am saying is that you must refrain from *judging* what you observe; refrain from making judgmental pronouncements about it; refrain from believing that you know exactly what's what in the whole scheme of things. The only way you can be a true agent of harmony is by being in constant attunement with the voice of God sounding within you, and by being in alignment with Source to receive and radiate a full flow of transformational Love as well as instructions for what to further do to bring the situation into harmony, something you simply cannot do when you are in judgment mode.

The way to bring harmony to any situation is to *raise its frequency,* and the way you do that is to add more Love. Disharmony cannot exist in the higher range of frequency; it cannot exist in the overwhelming presence of Love—the highest frequency. Wherever you perceive a situation as being out of harmony and you feel something needs to be done to change it, *it is an indicator that more Love is needed.* Though the typical human response to such situations has been with frequency-lowering, ego-based reactions such as indignation, judgment, and self-righteousness, that is the last thing that is needed. What is actually called for is *more Love.*

The highest and most powerfully effective action you can possibly take to harmonize and transform *any* situation is to increase the amount of Love and, thus, harmony, in it—letting the Great Mind of God sort out the details. If you focus on harmony and radiate Love from your heart, you will be doing the most transformational thing in your power to do. And it doesn't require knowing any details. Whether your perceptions are right on or not, you can never make a mistake doing that. Plus, when you are radiating Love, you are in the perfect position for receiving instruction from Spirit as to what else you are to do—what practical, effective, physical actions you can take—to further assist in transforming and harmonizing a situation.

I certainly don't recommend divorcing yourself from your feeling response of anger or hurt, or even fear, in any situation—indeed, unexpressed emotions are as damaging as inappropriately expressed ones. But I recommend that you feel your feelings as fully and as honestly as you can, and then place them on the altar of your heart and allow the Light of Love to transform them. Then use that newly realigned energy—that energy that now is pure Love again—to transform the situation you reacted to.

I don't advocate this "high road" out of some airy-fairy moral notion. If you understand Prime Principle, you know that what I recommend is simply practical. The only truly effective response to any situation is to radiate Love. Only by doing our job as unconditional transmitters of Love will we bring ourselves and all of humanity—indeed, all of Creation—back into harmony and up in frequency where we were meant to be.

EVERY TIME WE CHOOSE FEAR OVER LOVE, we empower the serpent. Every time we listen to the serpent within us instead of to God, we recreate the Fall. Every time we allow our lower nature to dominate us, we strengthen the schema for disharmony. If we are to reverse the process that started with Adam and Eve, and re-empower the schema for harmony and Wholeness, we must reestablish our correct relationship with God and close the frequency gap.

To close that gap between where you are currently dwelling and where you were designed to dwell, there is an aspect of *yourself* with which you must reunify. This aspect of you is purely divine and inviolable. It is the aspect of you that remains above the level of the magnetic gap in frequency and is perpetually aligned with Source. It is your gateway to the higher realms. It is your access to Eden.

CHAPTER FOUR

Your Spirit:
The Truth of You

*T*HOUGH YOUR EXPERIENCE OF LIFE MAY NOT HAVE ALWAYS REFLECTED IT, there is, indeed, a facet of you that has always been in perfect alignment with Source—and always will be. This entity has never been affected by the magnetic gap and therefore has never left Paradise. This part of you has never forgotten that It is inseparable from the Whole of Creation, or lost touch with Its divine nature. This aspect of you is who you are in truth. You are not the ego-centered being you may have always thought you were. You are Spirit, utilizing a human body.

One of the most tragic consequences of the Fall of Man is the loss of identity it caused humans to undergo. Once we departed from the vibrational level where Eden manifests, amnesia set in, causing us to forget who we are and why we are here. We have long believed that we are humans with spirits in us; when in fact, we are so much larger than that. We are divine, and it is time to own our actual identity once again and behave like the spiritual beings we are in truth.

In the process of recreating Eden, we will be waking up from the trance we've been in to remember who and what we are—not just at an intellectual level, but as a deep knowing. *This recognition comes automatically when you reach a certain level of frequency.* As your frequency rises, so does your consciousness and your ability to see higher.

Jesus of Nazareth knew who he was, and he called us to know the same about ourselves. Indeed, that was his mission on Planet Earth—not to be the *only* divine human exemplifying "the Father," but to awaken us to our own true identity as Spirit in human form, and to motivate us to behave accordingly. Because Jesus was operating at a high frequency, he was aware of his divinity. When we reach that level, we will be aware of ours, too. Those who maintain that it is heretical for humans to claim divinity are simply humans who have not yet reached the consciousness level of self-realization that only elevated frequency provides.

Since most of us are not yet sufficiently raised up to the level of frequency where we have experienced our divinity, and we are not yet fully merged with our Spirits, we are not at that place in consciousness yet that would allow us to view things purely through our Spirit's eyes to identify ourselves from the viewpoint of our divinity. Therefore, as a way to bridge where we are now in consciousness with where we are headed, I am going to speak of "you" as your current consciousness, and your Spirit as a *facet* of you. A sparkling, Light-filled, magnificent facet, indeed.

THE GRANDEST, MOST REAL AND ENDURING ASPECT OF YOU IS YOUR SPIRIT, who exists with or without your Earth suit on. Your Spirit manifested your body to provide itself with a vehicle to experience physical phenomena and to join the spiritual and physical worlds. So, you see, while your ego-self believes it can claim ownership of you, your life does not actually belong to your mind to do with as it pleases, at least not if you want to experience peace, harmony, and real joy. *Your life belongs to your Spirit.* But as you learn more about this amazing aspect of you, you will be happy—even eager—to relinquish ownership of your life. Your Spirit wants far greater, more gratifying, supremely thrilling things for you than your ordinary awareness can conceive of! In fact, allowing your Spirit to take over your life is the path to bliss and the very linchpin of the process of recreating Eden.

From a human perspective, let's look at your relationship with your Spirit in terms of the energy hierarchy. Your relationship with your Spirit is what positions you where you were created to be positioned in the Divine Design. Remember that the closer to the Core of Creation you get, the more concentrated the Life Force/ Love is. The concentration of Life Force Energy at the Core of Creation is inconceivably intense and the frequency so high, we cannot physically exist at that level. For human beings to partake of the Life Force from Source requires that we be connected up for just the right intensity. We must be positioned relative to it such that we receive the *optimal* flow for the way our bodies have been designed. Your Spirit is your interface with the higher levels of Being and brings you as close to the Core of Creation as is humanly possible to be. Your Spirit, therefore, positions you to effectively receive and utilize Source energy.

To understand this better, think of a mundane power source and how it operates. Imagine an electric power plant that harnesses energy from natural processes and then sends it forth as electricity. The electricity travels out via circuits to substations and transformers to be stepped down, distributed, and stepped down again to a form that can be utilized in homes and businesses for the operation of mechanical appliances. These appliances depend on this electrical power for their operation, requiring a prescribed amount of it, and are designed to interact with it in specific ways.

You certainly don't expect your iron or your TV to generate their own power, or to draw the electricity out of the air and use it to run themselves—at least not at our present stage of technological development. Nor do you expect them to operate with the high voltage directly from the main generator—they would burn up. To receive power they can use to operate most efficiently and effectively, according to their design, you know that they must be plugged into a circuit at the appropriate stage of the step-down process.

And so it is with you. You cannot generate your own power, even though your mind operates under the illusion that it can. You must have power from the Source, but you cannot sustain the high voltage *directly* from It. Your relationship with your Spirit connects you correctly with the "Main Power Plant," plugging you into the flow of energy at just the appropriate level for your optimal functioning. Like your iron or your TV, you can't expect usable power for yourself until you are properly "plugged in." Your Spirit positions you in the energy hierarchy at exactly the right point for you to thrive—*when* you are aligned with It.

Your Spirit is the highest frequency aspect of you. Below your Spirit in frequency are your mind and body, and above your Spirit are higher vibrational levels of Being, all the way up to the Core of Creation. Because of your Spirit's constant, perfect alignment with Source, It is perpetually at one with Great Spirit and Its frequency is never lowered. A flawless receiver and transmitter of the Life Force emanating from the Core, your Spirit is the channel through which Life Force from Source flows to you. All the Life Force/Love you will ever receive must come through your Spirit.

This flow from Source to you through your Spirit has been impeded, however. It is impeded at the level of your *consciousness*. That lethal magnetic gap to which we have been referring occurs on the energy spectrum between your Spirit and your consciousness. The problem with your alignment with Source has been that your ego-mind has been holding the rest of you separate from being unified with the frequency level of your Spirit. It has been sustaining a gap there. The goal, then, is to *close that gap by merging with your Spirit.*

We have already firmly established that we must be magnetically receptive to Source if we are to be aligned to receive a full, vitalizing flow of Life Force. The detail I have left out till now is that our receptivity to Source is designed to originate with receptivity to our own Spirits. Your Spirit is perfectly unified with Source and inseparable from It; therefore, It is always radiating (masculine mode), just as Source is. Therefore, to be correctly aligned with Source, you must be correctly aligned with your own Spirit by presenting your feminine (receptive) aspect of your mind to It.

How do you accomplish this? You allow your Spirit to take over your life. You honor your own Spirit as God, and you listen to and honor the guidance of your Spirit above all other input, trusting and obeying It in all matters. Simply put, you become totally available to your Spirit. Why? Because as a manifestation of the Greater Spirit, or God, your Spirit is, indeed, God-In-You. You exist to provide your Spirit with a viable presence in the material world. You exist to provide God an expression in human form. Only when you are aligned with your Spirit will the gates of Eden open for you. And only when you are aligned with your Spirit will you understand who you are.

I'M SURE YOU RECALL THE POINT IN THE STORY I told in the introduction about my visit to Eden where the voice within me announced, "I AM GOD." (If you skipped the introduction, now would be the time to go back and read it.) Because I assumed this voice was coming from my lesser self, my ego, trying to claim the glory of the Eden experience for itself, I renounced it and felt ashamed. Immediately upon doing so, I felt all the sublime energy that had buoyed me since I first turned my life over to God, drain out of me.

At first, I thought that the "irreverent" voice in my head claiming to be God was what caused the disconnection from the state of grace in which I had been existing for weeks. But after much prayerful meditation on it, and growth in my understanding of the entire experience, I finally recognized that the disconnection had not been caused by that at all. I hadn't experienced a frequency drop at the point where I heard "I AM GOD"—on the contrary, my energy had *surged* at that instant. It was only after I refused to accept what I'd heard, told myself I was "bad," and experienced the subsequent shame and humiliation, that I bottomed out.

I understand now that the frequency drop was *not* caused by my recognition of what I now know as the truth of who I AM, but was caused by my denial—indeed, my denouncement—of what I had heard within. The voice I had heard claiming divinity was not the voice of my ego, or the voice of some evil entity, but the *voice of my own Spirit*—an inseparable part of God, and the most real part of me. When the truth of my identity was announced in my mind, I was at that sublime point of finally having achieved unity with my Spirit and experiencing what it is to be the nexus between pure Spirit and "high-frequency human." I understand now that hearing "I AM GOD" was the most natural thing that could have happened considering the vibrational level where I was at the time it happened, in the realm of my Spirit; so very near to Eden.

Instead of rejoicing at the recognition of my innate divinity, I had allowed the commonly taught human notion that we are lowly beings and that God is a separate entity from us keep me from honoring what I was receiving firsthand from God. *That* is what sent me tumbling back from the realm of bliss into the old familiar world of strife and pain. The fear and shame I experienced, based in my acceptance of the faulty teachings about God that I had received from other humans during my Earth-indoctrination, is what had pulled the plug on the mighty flow of Life Force I had experienced in and through me, and is what had *actually* plunged me into despair.

Just as it happened to those first humans in the Garden of Eden, my honoring another voice over the voice of God sounding within me had ejected me from the gates of Paradise. It is the same failure to listen to and honor Spirit's voice within, the same self-judgment, the same refusal to know and acknowledge the truth of who we are, the same habit of allowing the voice of the serpent and the external world to trump the voice of Spirit, and the stubborn maintenance of our perception of being separate from God and all of Creation that keeps us in a perpetual state of energy drain and spiritual pain, locked out of the Garden. All the hardships, suffering, and misery on Earth are the result of those sorry human habits.

IF YOU, LIKE I, GREW UP IN THE JUDEO-CHRISTIAN TRADITION, you, too, probably internalized some version of the concept that God is a huge, super-busy part-man, part-magician, way up there somewhere, running the Universe. You know—the one whose favor you have to vie with everybody else for—that moody, fickle giant with the long gray beard and the list of everyone's good deeds and transgressions. Sometimes called "the man upstairs," this god bestows blessings and punishments at his whim—a kind of Santa Claus with a mean streak. Such a being is *limited,* but God is *unlimited*—not to mention ever so much more loving and accessible than that.

Yes, the genius of the Creator has provided you with your own personal, always available godhead. *God is in you.* How do you think that God can be everywhere at once? This is possible by virtue of Her/His existence in each living being. Of course, it is probably more accurate to say that *you* have been provided so that God can have a personal, always available human. From either perspective, it truly is a brilliant system—except that you haven't always been available to God the way God has been available to you! But we'll be getting into that further in a moment.

There are many who believe like I once did, that to conceive of any part of themselves as an aspect of God is to be disrespectful; that it somehow implies a diminishing of the power of God. Nothing could be further from the truth! Does acknowledging the existence of and appropriately utilizing the electrical outlet into which you plug your iron diminish the importance and tremendous power of the main electric generator? Or your respect for it? Of course not. And likewise, honoring your Spirit does not take one iota away from the greater God—or *Great* Spirit. In fact, being aware of this adds to God's effectiveness once you use the information to achieve proper alignment so you can be a more perfect expression of God's Love in the world.

If, even after reading the foregoing, you have a hard time fully accepting that God is in you—that you are God expressing as a human—it is perhaps because, based on the quality of your experience, it is difficult to believe that any part of you could be God-like. Because of this, you want to believe that God is outside of you, is better and more powerful than you are, and, certainly, is more reliable and consistently loving than you are. This is understandable since your primary experience of life has been on the "wrong side" of the magnetic gap. Your life has not been fully stewarded by your Spirit, but hijacked by your ego-driven mind, which, as we have seen, has been operating independently of your Spirit and has been primarily responding not to the Divine, but to the serpent and the imperfect world of its own creation—the schema for disharmony.

Not being in position to fully receive the constant stream of Love that is the very nature of God, or the wisdom and power of God, and with understandings based primarily on what relatively little it can observe from the misaligned external world instead of from the Whole of Creation, your mind as an independent entity is definitely limited, lacking in Love, and unreliable. Your ego-mind, sustaining the magnetic gap between your Spirit and the rest of you for much of your entire life, and keeping you at a lower frequency, has hardly fostered a recognition of the steadfast, unconditional nature of your perfectly aligned, totally loving Spirit, much less the knowing of your own divinity. No wonder you have felt powerless and have had so little sense of God-In-You.

But while your independently operating mind is limited, your Spirit, because of Its constant flawless receptivity to the higher-vibrational energy of Source and Source's unlimited Love and Wisdom, is *unlimited*. By virtue of Its position *above* the level of your renegade mind, your Spirit is *always* perfectly aligned with and inseparable from Source. Therefore, when the rest of you, in turn, is fully aligned with your Spirit to receive a steady flow of Love and Divine Wisdom, you will experience your unlimitedness. You will experience your innate Godliness and know who you are. There is nothing at all blasphemous about this. In fact, as I learned, the actual blasphemy is in refusing to acknowledge that you are an aspect of God and that, truly, *God is in you*. Only the serpent wants you to believe otherwise.

ACCORDING TO THE WAY YOU ARE DESIGNED, your Spirit is intended to be THE BOSS. Your mind exists for the purpose of creating and doing whatever your Spirit directs it to. Every thought, action, and bodily process is *rightly* preceded by spiritual impulse or command. This is designed to be one smooth, seamless operation with no lag time in between: Spirit impulses and your totally receptive, completely cooperative, Spirit-focused body-mind responds immediately in total obedience. Without hesitation and without question. And without first looking around to decide whether or not to obey based on the circumstances and data surrounding you. And certainly without checking to see what others might think of you!

When you override the messages or impulses of your Spirit and insist on operating from logic alone, accessing only the evidence available to your conscious mind through your senses, you frequently make decisions and take actions that are inconsistent with the Wholeness, and your resulting experience ranges from merely inconvenient to downright discordant. When, instead, you obey the impulses of your Spirit over the logic of your mind, you automatically attune with the Whole, and harmony and serendipity reign in your experience.

Let's consider an everyday example of this. Imagine that you are expecting important visitors to arrive from out of town for a few days' stay and you are getting ready to go out to the grocery store to stock up with special foods and to take care of several other errands relating to their visit. Your schedule is planned right down to the minute of their arrival, and if you are to get everything accomplished in time, it all has to go off like clockwork. Now let's say that as you are about to rush out the door, you suddenly think of your elderly friend, and a strong sense that you need to call her comes over you.

Instead of ignoring the urge and putting off the call until it is more convenient the way your logical mind is telling you to, you stop and call her (because, of course, you would never make a call while driving!). She says she has been feeling especially lonely and isolated and that your call has helped her immensely. As you are once more about to head out the door, the phone rings. It is your visitors calling to tell you that, due to an emergency, they will not be able to come.

If you had already left for your errands as scheduled, you would have missed this vital call and would not have known of the change in plans until you returned home. From the vantage point of the logical mind, you simply could not have known about these developments since your prospective visitors didn't know how to reach you away from home. But your Spirit, because of its greater vantage point, knew. The few moments you spent on the phone obeying your Spirit's inner urging and demonstrating love and compassion to your friend saved you a fortune in groceries you weren't going to need and the stress and time expenditure of running around doing errands that weren't necessary.

If you had overridden your urge to call your friend and relied, instead, on the "evidence" (which indicated that your visitors were definitely planning to come at a certain time and that fitting a phone call into your schedule would put you behind), you would have expended a lot of energy that would *not* have prospered the Whole, and parts of the Whole that were in need of your attention and energy would have gone lacking. And you probably would have been exasperated by all the money you spent needlessly, plus all the time you wasted, and may even have spewed out a few "toxic thoughts" over it all—which *certainly* would not have added to the sum-total of Love in the world!

In this particular example of obeying the voice of your Spirit, the only risk involved was that you might have inconvenienced your guests by not being home when they arrived, or that everything might not have seemed perfect the way your prideful ego would have preferred it to be. However, you will find that, even with much higher stakes, as you consistently obey your Spirit above all else, circumstances arrange themselves as if by magic so that everything works out. Whenever you align with your Spirit, you position yourself to coordinate with the Wholeness and raise your frequency, the reward of which is harmony at all levels.

Of course, the truth is that *not* obeying your inner voice is where the *real* danger lies. But because, more often than not, heeding your inner voice involves basing your actions on something as seemingly intangible and invisible as your intuition, your logic-loving, evidence-oriented, so-called rational mind finds itself totally out of its league. At the very least, your mind wants to *understand* what is going on, but it is simply not equipped to do so. It perceives a risk because it is not in control, and its belief that it must be in control is very strong.

That they are not the boss is certainly difficult for our ego-based minds to accept. They are used to being in charge—indeed, habituated to it—and believe that they *have* to be running the show for us to survive. To give up this position of dominance in our lives seems to the ego-based conscious mind to be an untenable risk, not to mention a comedown or a relinquishing of power. Because the Adam in you is aligned with the world of the serpent, he is greatly influenced by fear and survival issues. Thus, his fears control much of what he will and won't do. (This is ironic, since this low-frequency part of you is what ensures that you—the physical you, that is— really *won't* survive in the long run!) The true risk, of course, lies in Adam *not* relinquishing his illusions of power. Acting in its rightful position of "Chief Administrative Assistant" to the Spirit is where the *true* power of the mind lies. Just like any creation, it is most effective when it is used as it is designed to be used.

Don't confuse this with the notion that you are meant to suspend logic completely and *ignore* the world of your observations; obviously, the tools to monitor it and interact with it would not have been built into you if you were. It is simply that neither your logical mind nor the reverse-polarity world is to be your god. Instead, by virtue of your union with Source via your receptivity to your Spirit and the unified radiance this creates in you, you are not only meant to emanate Love out to the world in the same way that Source emanates Love to you, but you also are to perform specific tasks in the world that your Spirit communicates to you. Your mind is intended to facilitate this. In other words, you are designed to be God's presence in the world and provide stewardship for it, and *your powers of observation and reasoning are to be used in that capacity alone.*

Our minds are magnificent creations—perhaps the most magnificent of all creations. They literally have the capacity to influence and shape energy into any form imaginable—to create any conceivable reality—like compact versions of the Great Mind that created them, and that they are a part of. But as long as they continue to operate without the full guidance and resources of that

Great Mind via our Spirits, and until they quit using input from the reverse-polarity world, their creations—and our life experiences— are destined to be limited at best, grotesque at worst. Our minds must be aligned properly and working on behalf of Spirit in order to create Heaven on Earth—indeed, that is how it is done.

IMAGINE A GIGANTIC MASTER COMPUTER, a mainframe which contains all the intelligence in existence now or ever, every single solitary thing that there is to be known in the Universe, and changing every nano-second (faster, actually—I just don't have the vocabulary to express something faster than that!) to reflect the countless zillions of changes which are occurring throughout Creation at any given moment. This computer knows at all times how many grains of sand are on the beach (or in your tennis shoes), how many hairs are on (or off) your head, when a sparrow falls, whether you (or anyone else) is inhaling or exhaling, what the best route is to take on the way home from work, where to go to get any assistance you might need, what you need to do to create optimum health in your life, ad infinitum.

In a word, this computer knows *everything*—not just information we perceive as current, but every minute detail of what we perceive as history, and every minute detail of what we perceive as the future. In addition to containing complete knowledge of everything, it has the power to facilitate making any connections you might need. When you are properly aligned, it will orchestrate and manifest whatever that might be without you even having to ask! "It" is the Mind of God—and the Mind of God encompasses everything. *Everything.*

Having such a computer would certainly decrease the stress in your life, wouldn't it? Well, you *do* have such a computer. Your access point to all this is your Spirit—your "personal computer" or "PC"—which is connected with the "mainframe" via "modem." Not only is it linked up with the mainframe, it is networked with all the other PCs in existence. Just as you can access the mainframe and the Internet through your properly connnected PC to find out what you need to know, by relating properly with your Spirit, you can access the infinite knowledge and wisdom of Source and make decisions that will enhance all of Creation—while sparing yourself needless strife and inconveniences, as the following personal anecdote shows.

One blazing hot and sticky August day in my native state of North Carolina, I set out on a two-hour road trip with only enough gasoline to get me about forty-five minutes down the road. I planned to stop at a gas station I particularly liked that was about thirty minutes from the point where I had started out. I was cruising southward with my favorite driving tunes propelling me down the interstate, still a good fifteen minutes from my intended pit stop, and though the light on the gas gauge would be starting to flicker at any moment, I was intent on making it to that particular station.

Then something in my head said, "Take this exit and get gas!" Of course, my willful, ego-driven mind said, "I don't want to take this exit—I like the other station better. It's bigger and cleaner, the pumps have credit-card scanners, and I can get a snack there. Besides, I just got going—I don't want to break the momentum yet, and I have quite enough gas to get there." And the voice inside (which sounded exactly like me talking to myself, by the way) commanded, "Take this exit and get gas. NOW!"

I had, by this point, enough experience with listening and heeding my inner voice—and perhaps as importantly, with *not* listening and heeding it—to know that I'd best pay attention and do what I was being guided to do. So, somewhat grudgingly, I exited, got gas at the only place available—an old station with no modern conveniences, certainly no snacks I'd be willing to eat, and only one of its two pumps working—and headed back down the interstate. I had hardly made it a mile when I was forced to come to a dead stop behind what seemed to be an endless line of vehicles in all three southbound lanes. Due to a multi-car collision, as I was later to discover, the traffic was backed up for a couple of miles. We crept along, starting and stopping, for almost an hour before we finally cleared the wreck and the flow of traffic resumed—and before we reached another exit.

The accident had occurred between the exit where I was

"ordered" to stop and the next exit down the road. I would not have had enough gas to make it through the jam if I had not stopped when the voice within told me to. I'd have been stranded by the roadside in the brutal heat, and I would not have gotten where I was going till long after I needed to be there. Fortunately, I had been connected to the "mainframe" through paying attention, and had gotten advice based on what was known at a higher level than what my own mind could have known based on its observations or from any of the resources I had at hand. Thankfully, I heeded the voice within. It saved me a lot of trouble.

Everything you will ever need to know, be it mundane or spiritual, is available to you through your Spirit and its connection to the infinite Mind of God. Any question you will ever have is already answered there. All the guidance you will ever need for your life resides in the Mind of the One who created you—who better to tell you the path to travel to take you to your highest destiny? What better resource for finding out the specific tasks you were designed to accomplish in this world? Where better to find out the best strategies for healing and revitalizing the very body that It created than the Mind of the Creator? Who better to tell you the exits to take as well as the destinations to avoid?

Yes, listening and heeding God speaking to you via your Spirit and doing as you are guided is a critical factor in your realignment. It is vital to living a stress-free—or even a *reduced*-stress—life. It is something you were born knowing how to do, and it won't take you long to remember how, if you aren't well on your way to listening already. In the next chapter, we're going to look at just how to identify your Spirit's communications among all the messages coming at you from the world around you and from your own misaligned mind.

BESIDES BEING THE ADMINISTRATOR for the way that you can operate the most harmoniously within the Whole, your Spirit is the administrator of your health—of your wholeness. It knows everything about you. In a very real sense, It is the template for the material form of you. In addition to being the portal for the entry of Life Force into your body and being the access point to the awesome energy and intelligence of All That Is, your Spirit is the *pattern for your perfection*. The "blueprint" for the creation of the optimal version of you is your Spirit.

Before the physical part of you was born, your Spirit existed. As a perpetually perfectly aligned aspect of Great Spirit, the Source, It has existed for eternity. It is the part of you that was never born and *will never die*. As a mirror reflection of Its Creator, your Spirit is perfect and inviolable. It is the part of you that remains in the image and likeness of God no matter what may occur at the mental, emotional, or physical levels of your being.

All Life Force comes to you first through your Spirit. When your mind is properly aligned with It, allowing Life Force to flow in and circulate through you unimpeded, the energy is utilized according to Its original, intrinsic, perfect design for your optimal functioning. It is organized and routed through you according to the divine instructions contained within your Spirit. Acting as a pattern for the energy, your Spirit channels the Life Force in highly intelligent ways to create your total health and well-being.

As long as the energy is properly received by your body-mind and as long as the channels within it are not blocked, you are operating at optimal frequency where disease cannot exist and you are in a state of perfection that mirrors that of your Spirit. When the channels within your body-mind are blocked, your frequency drops, imbalances occur, the level of function within it diminishes, and you become ill, either to a greater or lesser degree. As long as we are not properly aligned with our Spirits, we are *all* ill—some of us have just already exhibited the symptoms; some of us haven't yet!

Only by allowing your Spirit to restore your body-mind to its original pattern of functioning can you be whole and well again. *This is what healing is. It is the removal of whatever is blocking the divinely patterned free-flow of Life Force through you.* Why do you think that sleep is so healing? It is because your conscious mind is "turned off" and Eve is able to realign with your Spirit for a vitalizing flow of Love to empower the pattern for perfection within you. Unfortunately, part-time alignment is not enough to keep you totally vital.

Thankfully, though, the perfection of this pattern and the capacity of your Spirit to channel the Life Force through you according to this pattern always remain intact, no matter your alignment. However, because your Spirit can only do this to the degree that you are properly aligned with It, you need to become fully realigned with your Spirit and allow the unlimited power of your Creator to clear the energy channels within you. Then you will be healed completely.

Healing—the process of becoming whole—is a feature that is built into the Divine Design. You will soon understand that intrinsic to Prime Principle is the key to healing at all levels; as we do what is necessary to rise in frequency and heal the magnetic gap, all else is healed—pulled into alignment—spontaneously.

BECAUSE YOU ARE SPIRIT EXPRESSING AS A HUMAN, the process of recreating Eden hinges on you bridging and closing the magnetic gap between your consciousness and your Spirit. Truly, this is a process of allowing your consciousness to become one with your Spirit so that there is no seam at all between your Spirit's thoughts and your thoughts, no difference between Spirit's motives and your own. In a very real sense your task is to merge with your Spirit—to become *one* with your Spirit in consciousness—the way you were designed to be.

While your ego-mind may be resistant to this notion, it needs to grok this: merging with your Spirit is the ticket to having all that you long for—all that you lost during your indoctrination to Earthlife. It is the antidote to stress and the assurance of living your life in harmony with the Whole. It is the healer within you that will restore your body and mind to radiant health when allowed to. It is the expressway to achieving your highest goals and the ticket to manifesting your heart's true desires. It is the path to fulfilling the Creator's highest purposes for you. It is the most necessary step in returning to Eden. It is, in a word, *everything*.

CHAPTER FIVE

A New Operating Procedure: Changing Your Mind

*N*OW THAT YOU UNDERSTAND THAT EVERY PART OF YOUR LIFE WILL BE HEALED AND ENERGIZED when you are fully aligned with Source by virtue of your relationship with your Spirit, and that you can access the blissful realm of Paradise by merging with It, you are probably raring to go. "Let's get this done *yesterday!*" you might be thinking. And doing so is, indeed, a simple proposition. But there is one small catch. Your healing can only be accomplished with the consent of the part of you that is causing you to stay misaligned. And it is quite invested in its current position.

As we established in the last chapter, the magnetic gap that partially separates you from the Source of Life Force occurs at the level of your conscious mind, which is still trying to act as the boss in your life. Therefore, it must be convinced to relinquish the status it has so long maintained for itself and accept that it is second, not first, in command. Fortunately, your conscious mind responds to what makes logical sense to it, and by now, it is probably starting to see the logic in coordinating with the Creator's Design for Harmony and Wholeness!

Let me refresh your memory about the advent of the ego and the dominance of this conscious, masculine aspect of the mind. If you recall, after the unfortunate incident in the Garden, a tragic reversal occurred between Adam and Eve, causing Adam to no longer get his information and energy exclusively from Spirit via Eve. Remember, God said that because of their disobedience, Adam (inner masculine, conscious mind) would henceforth rule over Eve (inner feminine, subconscious mind).

So, from then until now, Adam has *controlled* Eve: the inner masculine, for the most part, has controlled the inner feminine. And if the Adam side of the human magnet has control and wants to stay in reverse polarity, his flip side, Eve, is pretty much stuck. In addition to the multiple problems this causes due to operating counter to their design, the problem is compounded because, with Adam in control, the only way they could be restored is if Adam decided to *give up* control—and this is something he was no longer in position to comprehend the need for.

His view from his new position was one of separateness, as he no longer had his customary total union with the Wholeness. Adam, whom we can also call the "ego"—the part of us that sees separateness rather than oneness—now operated as if humans are stand-alone entities. Adam's actions, taken from that stance of separation and based not on inspiration but on the sensory-based information gathered from the misaligned world, information colored by the influence of the serpent—the fear-based, territorial, aggressive part of him—were most often inconsistent with the highest possibilities of harmony and, indeed, frequently created turmoil.

Adam's masculine-driven, ego-based agenda, which has dominated for eons, has created legions of humans out of harmony with the Whole and a world out of harmony—*seriously* out of harmony. As long as Adam refuses to let go of his alignment with reverse polarity, the magnetic gap prevails, peace eludes us, and the entities of reverse polarity continue to feast on the fallout.

Your mind, powerful by virtue of it being fashioned after the Great Mind of God, is creating your reality, just as our collective minds are creating our collective reality. The human mind creates by virtue of its patterning, input, and passion. The aligned mind creates from Oneness-consciousness and the schema of Wholeness and harmony with the input it receives from Spirit, according to higher-frequency thought-patterning, and it fuels its creations with Love. Thus, the creations of the aligned mind are of high frequency, too, and, of course, in harmony.

But the misaligned mind creates from the standpoint of separateness, according to lower-frequency thought-patterning, with the input it receives through the senses from the misaligned world around it. It fuels its creations with emotional energy aligned with fear. Thus, the misaligned mind creates a reflection of itself—a world out of harmony, often *way* out of harmony—vibrating at a corresponding lower frequency, and manifesting forms and cultural entities that behave accordingly. Until Adam chooses to realign so that the input from which the human mind creates is from the realm of Oneness and harmony, humanity is in a pickle!

Of course, this is why your own world—your personal life experience—is out of harmony as well. The backward dynamic of the inner masculine dominating the inner feminine is still playing out in your own mind to a greater or lesser degree depending on your progress in releasing your life to your Spirit. Instead of Eve and Adam being constantly available to take the energy from Source and use it to create according to divine impulse (as the sequence was designed to work), now the Adam in you far too frequently keeps your mind out of alignment, causing it to create according to the input received from the world of separation, fear, and disharmony.

And as they say in the computer world, "garbage in, garbage out." Happily, you, as the operator, have the choice to change where your input is coming from.

So the bottom line is that your ego—the Adam aspect of you which is still calling the shots—must *make the decision* to let go of its faulty positioning. He must honor Eve's rightful place in the scheme of things and let her do her job, and he must act on the orders from Spirit coming through Eve, thus empowering your mind to operate as it was created to. There must be a holy balance of

71

your inner feminine and inner masculine *working in right order* if your life is to be harmonious. And only when this happens at the individual level will we see it reflected in the world at large where the evidence of the tragic breakdown of their relationship is so graphically evident. Only when your inner Adam is sufficiently convinced to release his death grip on his alignment with reverse polarity can the necessary balance be restored at every level of your world.

The challenge here is one that, hopefully, this book has helped you with. You must assist your logic-loving ego-mind—the Adam in you—in understanding why it is eminently logical for it to re-align and what the benefits of doing so are! While it may seem that your logical mind is somewhat the villain in this whole mess, the truth is, it is just an entity that is misinformed about its role and purpose, not to mention its rightful status. It is useless to blame your ego for its devotion to running your life, maintaining the illusion of separateness, and creating according to its faulty input. It mistakenly believes that your very survival depends on it carrying on as it always has and is doing the best it can with its limited abilities.

If you recall, during your Earth indoctrination, your conscious mind was given the responsibility of taking care of you, of guiding you and providing for you because your caretakers had lost touch with how the Creator's Design for Harmony and Wholeness is engineered. But, try as it might, there is no way your misaligned ego-mind can steward your life in harmony, ease, and joy—something your Spirit can do effortlessly. The mind no longer under the dominion of Spirit is an entity striving to do something for which it was not created. Once it understands that, it may just start to let go in utter relief! It may be willing to turn loose before it completely falls apart—something many minds do in this modern age of constant stress.

Your mind needs to understand that it was never designed to run your life. It is not equipped to do the job it has so valiantly been struggling to do. The mental picture I get when thinking of the human mind attempting to fulfill the position that rightly belongs to Spirit is an old film image of a gigantic early computer confronted with a task too large and complex for its capabilities—you know, the one where the mad scientist with the wild hair is inputting more and more data till the computer begins quaking, shorts out, starts to spark and smoke, and finally falls apart. Your mind is just as overwhelmed trying to do what it was not designed to do, yet still it soldiers on, thinking this is just the way things have to be.

Because it has allowed you to read this far, however, your mind might, indeed, be ready to begin the process of relinquishing its illusions and letting go of the reins. Likely it has already recognized that change is called for. Certainly, when it comes to the full realization that being second in command means ease and harmony instead of the constant exhausting struggle it currently endures, it will begin to defer to the authority of your Spirit.

One way to initiate the process is to express your intent to surrender to the dominion of your Spirit. Your Spirit really doesn't need you to do this, but your mind certainly does! Expressing your intent is helpful to inform your mind-body complex that a change is taking place—to inform it that your Spirit is henceforth to reign supreme. You can accomplish this by creating and performing a surrender ritual that can be as simple as prayerfully making a brief but sincere statement acknowledging your Spirit as being in charge and your mind as its assistant, or it can be as elaborate as you wish it to be. (Just don't make it so elaborate that it is too much trouble to follow through on—your mind may just seize on any excuse not to relinquish power!) This "declaration of dependence" on your Spirit is a potent way to initiate your newly changed relationship with God-In-You.

One vital component in this surrender process is *thanking your mind* for its amazing service, its unflagging devotion to your survival, and its valiant attempts to bring your life into harmony in the face of the impossibility of it ever succeeding without the guidance of your omniscient Spirit. I am certain of one thing—when your conscious mind truly and fully perceives what its rightful position is relative to Spirit, and how much easier things will be in that aligned state, it will jump on the bandwagon with gusto. Your mind is *tired*—tired of trying to do a heroic job against all odds, a job it was never designed to do. Can't you just feel how exhausted it is? It will be so much more energized and effective once it lets go and lets your Spirit make its job easy!

Be aware, however, that a true consciousness of surrender will likely need to be practiced consistently until it takes hold as your *modus operandi.* You will need to be vigilant as it is so easy to fall back into the habit of seeking to control things at a mental level. In fact, you are likely to need to remind yourself to release things to your Spirit many, many times a day—as many times a day as you notice that things are not flowing smoothly and easily. If this sounds like a lot of work, remember that it is much less work than dealing with the messes you make by letting your limited, independently operating mind lead you! Once your mind sees over and over again how much more smoothly your life runs with your Spirit in charge, surrender will become spontaneous and your life will become more and more harmonious and free of stress. Toward the end of this chapter, I will share with you a technique I often use when I realize the need to realign myself, allow my Spirit full ownership of me, and radiate Love.

MY HOPE IS THAT YOU DO NOT HAVE TO COME TO THE END OF YOUR ROPE in order to be convinced to make the necessary changes in your life. But it has certainly been my experience that nothing succeeds quite like being in dire straits to get your attention, convince you to give up the old, ineffective way of operating, and allow your Spirit to take over! If you recall, I came to the point of surrendering to the Divine Design via just such a desperation route.

I was dealing with an excruciatingly painful, "incurable" disease and was becoming more crippled every day. Nothing that I—or anyone in the medical community—had come up with to try to halt the disease process was doing any good at all and, in fact, was making things worse. I was weakened from taking handfuls of prescription medications I sensed were poisoning me, and I was exhausted from months of futilely trying to figure it all out. The final blow had come when it seemed that even the natural methods I had started to look into, and had such high hopes for, would not be able to reverse the damage I had done to my body with the corticosteroids I had become addicted to, prescribed by the first of the many doctors from whom I had sought help.

At my wits' end (quite a powerful place to be, as it turns out) and completely terrified, I finally let go of the struggle to figure out a solution to my problems and gave up. I even spontaneously announced out loud, "I give up! I can't do this anymore." And then I heard a little child's voice coming from me, imploring the only version of God I understood at the time—a sort of all-powerful, magical Daddy-God in a faraway heaven—to help me. I begged for help for a minute or two, wailed loudly for awhile, and when I ran out of tears and energy, the proverbial "peace that passes understanding" took over. I fell asleep, and that was that. When I woke up the next morning, amazing things began to happen. My ascent to Eden, which took place over the next couple of months, was underway.

In my years of trying to fully understand how the whole thing happened, I believe I have pegged the main components that went into this successful surrender experience. (Any resemblance to steps in a twelve-step program is purely coincidental—or is it?)

First, I came to the realization that my problems were unsolvable at the human, mental level. Second, I completely and utterly gave up on trying and stopped working to figure out a solution. Third, I acknowledged that, while my human capabilities were *not* able to solve my problems, there was, indeed, a power equal to the task. Fourth, I tapped into the innocent, naive aspect of myself— the innocent, totally unsophisticated, *trusting* child-self, who, while a little misled about where God resides, had, nonetheless, never lost touch with the innate knowing that there is an omnipotent power that can make miracles (or what we think of as miracles) happen.

I now realize that begging was unnecessary. I didn't have to convince God to help me—God In Me had been waiting patiently for me to get to the point where I'd let go and let God take over, just as God-In-You is waiting for you to get there, too! But the begging, wailing, and carrying on were probably helpful in exhausting me so that I didn't have the energy to take back up the mental load I had finally laid down. It also served to release all the tension from my body and mind so I was relaxed enough to receive all the Love that my Spirit was pouring forth to me.

I certainly could not have predicted what would come of what began as the most stressful, lowest point of my life. In only an hour or so, I went from utter despair to a peace of mind I had never known possible. Remarkably, although the same set of circumstances existed externally at this point, the burden was gone and everything had changed. I was totally relaxed for what seemed like the first time in my life! I felt inexplicably joyful and overflowing with Love! Whereas I had felt dark, heavy, tense, fearful, and deeply conflicted when the event began, I felt light, happy, and supremely calm by the time I had finished wailing out all my stress. Oddly, though I had no new ideas about how to solve my problems, I was somehow certain that everything would be all right.

Why did that event produce a sense of calm euphoria in me? These many years later, I understand that my spontaneous surrender and laying down of my burdens had shot my frequency up—way up—to the level where peace reigns and joy is the norm. By allowing a restoration of myself to the original positioning humans were designed to occupy in relation to Spirit, I had launched myself to a level of being I had not experienced since I was a carefree baby. My knowing that everything was going to be okay, despite the external evidence to the contrary, was the logical outcome of being reunited with the divine, omnipotent aspect of me.

As I experienced the dramatic increase of Love through my new alignment with Spirit, my natural response was to radiate the Love that was now filling me up and overflowing. This was the beginning of what was to be a great love affair between me and my Spirit. The more Love I experienced flowing through me, the more Love I felt for my Spirit (which I then just characterized as "God") and the higher my frequency became. My love for my Spirit flowing out of me seemed to touch and transform everyone and everything around me!

I see now that this is because *Spirit is in everything.* The way the Whole of Creation is designed, our love *for* Spirit—the natural response to Love *from* Spirit—does not return directly back inward to the Core of Creation. Instead, it continues outward on the rays of the energy hierarchy, radiating and being received by the Spirit in all Creation, and loops back around to be drawn back to the Core of Creation again. (This is where that bagel metaphor I mentioned comes in!)

Your primary job as a human being is to radiate Love. As you do, you not only radiate Love out to the world around you; you continue the natural cycle of Love that emanates from the Core of Creation through that over which you have dominion in the energy hierarchy, which is everything below you in frequency. This Love that you radiate blesses all in sequence and then cycles back to the Core. Expediting the natural "journey" of the Love that is radiated to you back to the Heart of God, the Core of Creation, is the very system in which you were born to participate, and when you do it consistently, Eden is your home. What an exquisite design!

Yes, letting Love radiate from you constantly so that the cycle of Life Force is completed without interruption is the task you were designed for. Letting Love radiate without any agendas or conditions is the key. Now I'm going to say something that may at first seem contradictory—something that may even shock you. Unconditional love—that highest of spiritual goals—is a bogus concept, at least as it is normally defined and attempted!

It's difficult to love somebody who is being cruel. It's difficult to love someone who is ignorantly doing damage to your world. It's especially difficult to love anyone or anything when you're uncomfortable or out of sorts! But if there is one thing that I have learned about the genius of our Creator, it is that Creation is based on *ease.* If it's *difficult,* it is not a part of the Creator's Design for Harmony and Wholeness—or, at least, the hard way of going about it is not in the Design. Loving everything and everyone unconditionally—despite their shortcomings and despite whatever of them is in reverse polarity—is just too, too hard for human beings to do for more than a minute at a time, especially with their judgmental, separation-oriented logical mind in charge. *That is why it is not a requirement!*

What *is* required is that you *love Spirit*. That you allow the Life Force flowing through you to fill you up, to raise you up in frequency, and that you let your great, *natural* love response for Spirit—the Spirit that is not only the truth of you but is the essence of everyone and everything—overflow and, thus, radiate from you so that it blesses all as it continues its journey back to the Heart of God.

As Jesus, the master teacher and perfect example of a divine human, taught, "Thou shalt love the Lord thy God with all thy heart, and with all thy soul, and with all thy mind." [1]

If you are busy loving God with all of you, there is nothing left with which to love anything lesser (or what you *perceive* as being lesser)! Does this mean you should not love your less-than-perfect but completely endearing husband? Your mischievous, but nonetheless wonderful, child? Your irritating neighbor? Not at all. Love them with all your being! But be aware that what you're really loving is the God in them. The Love you experience toward anyone is the Love moving through you by virtue of the Love response that originates with Spirit and is being magnetized back to Spirit.

The *only* Love you feel is God's Love moving through you. The Love you experience in response to "others" is Love that God In Them magnetizes and draws *through you* as a part of the natural progression of Love through its cycle, *or* that God-In-You is drawing *through you*, from them, in completion of a cycle. In a very real sense, though you may feel affection for personality aspects of them, it is God In Them that you actually love, God In Them that is drawing forth your Love, and God In Them that expands by virtue of your Love. Always remember that Love comes only *from* God and returns only *to* God—and God—Spirit—is in everything.

While it is hard to love many things in this misaligned world, it is *supremely easy* to love Spirit when you are filled up to overflowing with the Love *from* Spirit! It is the most natural thing there is!

---

1 Matthew 22:37, New Testament of the *Holy Bible,* King James Version.

Your mandate, then, is simply to love Spirit. The rest of the cycle will occur naturally! While seeking the God in everyone is a way to remind yourself of your Oneness, you don't have to search to see the God in someone so that you can love them. You don't need to struggle to love the "unlovable." You merely need to love your own Spirit, who is inseparable from the Greater Spirit—the Spirit in all— and, by so doing, the Love and harmony in all things is increased. I hope that is as much of a relief to you as it was to me when it finally became clear!

BACK TO THE CHALLENGE OF GETTING THE LOGICAL, MASCULINE ASPECT of your mind on board with the plan of letting Spirit rule. In the process of understanding how that is done, I thought of meditation and how effective it is at realigning you so that the Love from your Spirit can flow through you unobstructed—how meditation opens the channel for wisdom from the Great Mind of God to flow to you. But if you have ever meditated, you know how great the challenge is in getting your conscious mind to *let go*—to get it to relax, go dormant so to speak, and release its grip on its faulty positioning so that the "wheels" of your mind can be reversed and the proper sequence of flow can take place from Spirit through to your subconscious.

As effective as meditation is—and for that matter, as effective as *sleep* is—at getting your mind out of the way so you can be in proper alignment at least some of the time, *inactivity* is antithetical to the nature of the inner masculine, *action-loving* logical mind. While a relaxation of the logical mind is surely called for, it just is not natural for it to be "turned off." Turning it off—getting it out of the way— is a useful substitute measure, but it just isn't how it is designed to work on a regular basis. And we've already discussed how difficult it is to change something's basic nature.

I have come to understand that the Creator made no mistakes whatever in designing our "equipment." If we have a mind that thrives on action—and we surely do—it is ineffective and futile to fight that. What we need to do is start using its very nature to achieve the goal of getting it on board with the new regime! Instead of trying to turn it off, we simply need to enlist it! In order to get your mind to move from the backward action of trying to run things according to an ego-based, separatist agenda, your mind needs to be engaged in *the kind of action it was designed for* instead.

This brings to mind the chicken and the egg conundrum—until you're properly aligned, how do you know what kind of action your Spirit wants you to be engaged in? This you can always count on: No matter what other action is ever called for by your Spirit, it's for sure that radiating Love constitutes correct action and sets up the correct sequence of energy movement through you. It is the baseline activity for you—the one any other activity is meant to be an enhancement of. And you can radiate Love by *deciding* to.

While the logical mind is not the source of Love, and a nozzle control at the end of a garden hose is not the source of water, you can start the flow of either one from those levels, particularly since they are the very things blocking the flow! Just like the flow of water has already been initiated by the time it gets to the hose nozzle, so the flow of Love is just waiting to be able to complete its journey via correct alignment. When your logical mind decides to engage in consciously radiating Love, correct alignment is assured as it necessitates that there be the overflowing Love moving through you so it can be radiated!

When I first experienced Love filling me up and overflowing from me, it was certainly not something I was doing intentionally at a conscious level—it occurred due to the spontaneous surrender I had naively undertaken. But I quickly noticed that whenever I felt overwhelming love for my Spirit, it lifted me up and made me feel even more wonderful. So, wanting some more of that ecstasy, I instinctively began to "turn it on" on purpose! I discovered that loving my Spirit intentionally was a powerful way to realign myself. By engaging my oh-so-eager conscious mind in the very activity it was designed to facilitate, I learned I could achieve the same effect.

The more I intentionally loved my Spirit, the more I felt my Spirit loving me. The more I experienced this "on purpose," the more I spontaneously felt the Love from my Spirit. The more I let go to It, the more I experienced my Spirit guiding me to a smoother path and solving my problems. As long as I kept completely trusting and loving my Spirit, and doing as I was guided to do, the phenomenon not only continued, it escalated. I was climbing higher and higher in frequency and experiencing joy as a constant. A mere coincidence? I don't think so!

Built into you is not only the mental equipment for initiating the flow, but the physical and emotional equipment for intentionally raising your frequency, too. Elevated frequency is a result of correct alignment, but you can engage in purposely raising your frequency by your conscious intention, using the equipment -installed in you to do so. Since it simply can't be done without correct alignment, your intention and action pull you into correct alignment.

The feeling response to being filled up with Love from your Spirit is joy. Higher frequency energy—Love—activates a joy response in your emotional body. I like to say that joy is a frequency—but it is more accurate to say that joy is your emotional response to higher frequency. When you are at a certain frequency, feeling the Love *from* Spirit moving through you *to* Spirit, the natural feeling you have is joy. And here is something truly empowering to know: when you feel joy, you are at a higher frequency.

Why is that so vital? If you want to raise your frequency, *feel* joy! You can *decide* to feel the joy that loving your Spirit puts you in touch with! You can create the feeling of joy within your emotional body, and it will shoot your frequency up. While most of us go through life believing that we can only experience emotions in response to an external energy stimulus, the truth is that we can make the *choice* to feel joy. This will be a totally moot point once you are realigned and constantly radiating Love as you were designed to because joy—no, *ecstasy*—is the emotional response to the level of frequency you experience when you are back in Eden. But between now and then, you may experience a moment or two where you need to raise your frequency!

How do you cause yourself to "feel" joy? You deliberately turn it on by *remembering* what joy feels like and allowing your body to take on the physical sensations of joy. You know, that giddy feeling that occurs when you are truly joyful? That close-to-tears—happy tears—feeling? That buzz you feel when you are joyful? That magnificent, expansive feeling you have when you first fall in love? The amazing feeling you have when you first meet your newborn child? The thrill you get from a stirring piece of music? Use your capacity to remember what that *feels* like and then replicate that feeling in your body! Feel the energy rising up and intensifying! Recreate the physical sensation of the butterflies-in-the-stomach, about-to-burst excitement. Enhance it with your breathing—and you are there! You are in the "joy space." *You are in the vibrational realm of your Spirit, experiencing the response to Love.*

As you rise up in frequency toward the level of your Spirit—toward merging and becoming one with your Spirit—you will be spontaneously joyful. As you are in this state more and more, your normal emotional state will default to joyousness! You will no longer need to be joyful "on purpose"—you will experience that as your foundational state. In the meantime, you can move closer to your Spirit by simply *deciding* to and then *feeling* it. Isn't that cool? Yet another way your action-oriented mind can participate in getting you where you long to go!

Sometimes you may need some help in deliberately going to the joy space, and the Creator has provided many tools to help with that. I find that music, particularly happy, lively music that was created in a consciousness of Love, can shoot my frequency up faster than just about anything. I also find that aromatherapy, using the highest-quality essential oils—not perfume oils or synthetic fragrances, but natural plant oils from organically grown herbs and flowers distilled in ways that maintain their life force—are immensely helpful in raising my frequency. Dancing, playing, exercising, vocalizing, creating—anything that gets your energy moving is great for raising your frequency and catapulting you into joy. And it is hard to beat being out in Nature on a beautiful day, loving Mother Earth, and feeling her love you in return, for setting up the environment in which it is easy to access joy! There are a myriad of ways to elevate your vibrational level and once you set your intention to it, your Spirit will guide you toward them.

There is one sure-fire way to be in harmony with the Whole and lift yourself—and perhaps someone else—upward toward the joy space that deserves special mention: expressing Love by doing something ego-less* for someone. Indeed, when you perform an ego-less act, you are acting purely on behalf of your Spirit, doing something for someone with no prospect of receiving anything in return (other than a rise in frequency!). If you've ever experienced, or even just heard of, a "volunteer's high," this is what is behind it. Doing something for someone without expecting anything back aligns you properly and raises your frequency. A caveat, though: Expecting *anything*—including a certain result, or even just a little appreciation—takes an act out of the category of being ego-less and diminishes its frequency-raising power!

When you deliberately create the sensation of joy to rise up to the realm of your Spirit's higher frequency, you disengage from the schema for disharmony and align more completely with the schema for harmony. Even if sometimes you find it a challenge to completely disentangle from reverse polarity to rise up to the joy space, it is powerful to even intend to do so, as it is the first step in the process. While it may not always rocket you immediately into the heart-leaping-up, butterflies-in-your-stomach joy space, it will withdraw enough of you from the schema for disharmony to begin to raise your frequency, and once you initiate that, the process *will* unfold.

IN THE LAST CHAPTER, THE TOPIC OF COMMUNICATION WITH YOUR SPIRIT CAME UP. Granted, when you are constantly radiating Love, and thus in perfect alignment, you won't need any guidance in this—your consciousness and your Spirit's impulses will be so closely aligned, all your thoughts will accurately reflect your Spirit's will. Even though I'm eager to be completely optimistic and would love to believe that reading this book is going to immediately catalyze you into a

---

2 I'm using the term "ego-less" instead of "selfless" for a reason. Far too many of us believe that we are to do things for others at the *expense* of ourselves, but the type of action I'm talking about enhances *both* the giver and the receiver.

permanent merge with your Spirit, it's certainly possible that this state of total oneness won't be reached overnight for most! So, in the meantime, let's look more closely at this idea of guidance from your Spirit.

As we begin to release ourselves to our Spirits and let the divine part of us take over, we need to turn over our very lives to the stewardship of our Spirits. "Let go and let God" is a saying you have probably heard before, and it pretty much sums up what we are talking about here. Just as I surrendered my declining health and medical nightmare to Spirit and received impeccable guidance that led me to healing at all levels, we have to learn to surrender *everything* in our lives to the stewardship of God-In-Us. Our health, our relationships, our finances, our safety—no matter what the challenge is, your Spirit knows exactly what is needed and can facilitate the ideal solution.

I want to make it clear at this juncture that I am not suggesting you turn over your problems to your Spirit and then just hide out in a cave till something changes. Not at all. Remember that your Spirit is meant to *direct* your life, thoughts, and actions—but your mind and body are its soldiers. And as I said, your logical, action-oriented mind is not going to sit idly by! It needs a job—it needs specific ways to serve your Spirit in addition to the baseline activity of radiating Love. Once you turn something over to your Spirit, you can expect to be prompted as to the steps you must take to do what is necessary to bring the situation into harmony. You are to take those steps, knowing that God-In-You is guiding you to a solution that prospers you as a part of the Whole.

Don't expect that this guidance will come as an outline with points A, B, and C, though anything is possible! More likely, it will require that you take each step without knowing what the next step will be, and not always really knowing why you are doing what you are doing, just feeling compelled from within to do so. You can trust that your Spirit is of the highest integrity, operating from the highest possible wisdom, and is always seeking to prosper you as an integral aspect of the Whole of Creation.

Your ego, while also always looking out for your best interests, or rather, what it *thinks* your best interests are, seeks merely to prosper you as if you are a stand-alone entity. But you are not, and you can only truly prosper when the prosperity of the Whole of Creation is taken into consideration. Your ego just doesn't have the right positioning to be able to see what is actually the highest possible path, but your Spirit does.

Sometimes, the guidance you receive from your Spirit may not make a lot of sense to your logical mind, looking at things from its limited viewpoint, or the guidance may even *seem* to your logical mind to be downright antithetical to what you wish to accomplish. But when you follow the guidance of your Spirit anyway—knowing that as you act in good faith, the result is a closer alignment with your Spirit, success in meeting whatever your challenge is, and of course, greater harmony—that is what becomes the reality. *When you trust completely and at all times that, with Spirit in charge, all is in Divine Order and is working out harmoniously, it becomes your reality!* And the more you believe that, amazingly, the more evidence there will be for your evidence-hungry mind to *see* that it is so.

Your Spirit is continuously beaming communications to you. As long as your mind is properly receptive to your Spirit, this vital communication is received. But if your mind is busy being distracted by its fascination with the world that serves the ego, or by the fear-based broadcasts of the lower self, the communications are not received—or the signals are fuzzy at best. Like a radio broadcast that takes place regardless of who is listening, your Spirit is constantly broadcasting to you, but you can only receive that broadcast if your radio is tuned to the right station and you are paying attention.

Of course, in addition to paying attention and being open and receptive to the wellspring of information coming to you through your Spirit, you need to understand Its language and have confidence in it. Because this language is personal between you and your Spirit, you are the only one who can unlock its secrets through attention and experience. It is not something that someone can give you a special decoder for! There are some generalizations I can offer you, though.

Sometimes the language of your Spirit is verbal, as it was when

I heard, "I AM GOD" and "Take this exit!" More often, it is presented in a nonverbal format. This language of your Spirit, regardless of the form it takes, is what we are accustomed to calling *intuition* and can usually best be described as a *knowing*. It may take the form of an urge, an impulse, a feeling, a dream, a vision, a song you can't get out of your head, a bodily sensation, a voice—pretty much the sky's the limit on your Spirit's resources for getting through to you.

Your Spirit will often give you information via books, movies, information you find on the Internet, spiritual teachers, and even from the mouths of your husband, your mother, your baby sister, complete strangers—pretty much anybody—even people you don't like! (Of course, these "mouthpieces for Spirit" often have no clue that's what they are.) Your Spirit knows you intimately and will use any means necessary to deliver Its messages, and sometimes those means are extremely creative—sometimes they *have* to be!

One of the main channels of communication your Spirit uses is your imagination, and while your logical mind may not have a properly high regard for it, your imagination is one of your divine tools for connecting to the wisdom of the Great Mind of God. Your fearful self likes to use the imagination, too, for dreaming up frightening scenarios and creating chaos, but it is not hard to discern the difference in energy between your Spirit's messages and the messages that arise from reverse polarity.

I can almost hear you asking this next question: How *do* you know for sure which messages are from your Spirit and which are from your ego or some other lesser, untrustworthy part of you? And which messages are your Spirit speaking through your mother and which messages are simply from your mother? (And yes, your Spirit trumps even your mother in the message hierarchy!) First and most obviously, when it is a message from your Spirit, it is higher in frequency. For this and many other reasons, you will need to learn how to sense and monitor frequency.

You were sent to Earth with both *mental* and *physical* equipment for gauging frequency, for discerning things that are in harmony and aligned with Spirit, and those that are not. Though these tools have been largely decommissioned since you arrived on Earth, it is time to recommission them in service to your Spirit. To develop the ability to recognize the truth coming to you via your Spirit and differentiate it from the ideas coming from a lesser source, learn to pay close attention to what goes on inside your mind and body in relationship to energy, to frequency.

One of the most important frequency-monitoring skills to develop is the ability to sense when your frequency rises and when it drops. When you are aligned with your Spirit, your frequency is high due to the increase of Life Force/Love that alignment provides. Likewise, when you attune to the voice of your Spirit, you will experience a rise in frequency. When you are attuned with something lesser, your frequency will drop. Your Spirit's messages will always be of a high frequency.

Your emotions are excellent monitors of the integrity of energy, and ideally, you can tell by your emotional response whether energy is in harmony or not. I need to add a caveat here, though. While our emotional bodies are designed to accurately monitor energy, most of us are so emotionally congested, we can't always get completely accurate readings. At this point, your emotions aren't reliable enough to depend on for gauging energy—at least not solely. As we recover our energy-moving abilities, this will improve, but in the meantime, developing your ability to sense the rising and falling frequency within your physical body will be of utmost importance.

When the idea or message is coming to you through your Spirit, you may feel an excitement, a lightness, an openness, a sense of peace, or perhaps a jolt of energy such as a sensation of heat in your solar plexus or a swelling of Love in your heart. You may have the sense that a puzzle piece has clicked into place. Or you may at first be unaware of feeling anything at all. Mentally, you may even experience some resistance.

So often our logic-loving, "it's not real unless I can see it and it's not valid unless it fits in my box" minds will try to prove that ideas from Spirit are threatening or illogical, but with careful observation, you will know when that is going on. It is natural for your ego-self to try and prevent you from taking a path that looks to it to be risky, but when you devote yourself to following your inner guidance, the fire of your Spirit will ultimately raise you up to over-come the fear and propel you forward—if it is in alignment with the Creator's Design for Harmony and Wholeness. Your Spirit is always steering you toward the higher path.

On the other hand, you may find that when the idea or message you are considering is *not* coming through your Spirit, or if your Spirit is trying to steer you away from something, you feel a drop in your overall energy. Remember that when you are receptive to anything other than your Spirit, there is a drop in frequency as you are out of alignment and Life Force is lessened. You may feel a shutting down, a closing in, an uncomfortable feeling in your solar plexus, a sense that there's a dark cloud present, perhaps a kind of a sticky "thickness" to the energy, or a special signal that you'll come to recognize with experience. Or you just may have that nag-ging feeling that something isn't right. You may notice that when your thinking is out of harmony with the Whole, your body just feels weaker, less alive. Remember that when you are not aligned with your Spirit, your energy—the Life Force moving through you—is diminished.

Another clue for discerning if a communication is coming from your Spirit is that your Spirit is all about ease and simplicity. Mes-sages from your Spirit will be simple and elegant as are all things of higher frequency. If what you are getting is heavy, complex, compli-cated, or convoluted, it is likely that the message is not purely from your Spirit. Most probably, your mind has presented an answer with-out your Spirit's guidance, or has added its own, not necessarily ac-curate take on top of your Spirit's divine guidance. While one of your logical mind's jobs is to take what your Spirit tells it and convert it into concrete form, it needs to first allow the energy of it to trip the right mental triggers, not just impatiently grab the message and ap-propriate it to support its own limited ideas. As you grow in your relationship with your Spirit and raise your frequency, this pure trans-lation will be instantaneous. For now, just be aware that your logical mind isn't always trustworthy the way your Spirit is!

Your Spirit's voice will never guide you to do harm to anyone—either in a direct or indirect way—and will always guide you to-ward greater integrity. Though you may be called upon to speak out or act in ways that challenge the status quo or make the ego-selves of others uncomfortable, your Spirit's voice will never tell you to do something that will cause damage to anyone. While you've probably heard of psychotic people who, after committing a hei-nous act, say that "The voices told me to do it," or even "God told me to do it," you can be assured that the voice they were heeding was not their Spirit's. As I have found, my Spirit's voice sounding within me sounds just like me talking to myself. If you are hearing a voice or voices that don't sound like you, you will want to double check that what you are hearing is, indeed, a message from your Spirit.

If, after applying all the foregoing, you are in doubt about the origin of any internal communication, make a firm declaration that you will only heed instructions from your own perfectly aligned Spirit; declare that you are only willing to respond to energy com-ing through your Spirit, and that you will ignore anything lesser. Making such a declaration on a regular basis, such as before you ask your Spirit for guidance on any matter or just as a way to start your day, can expedite your realignment with your Spirit, raise your frequency, and make clear communication easier—and keep the serpent's input out of your internal conversations!

Keep in mind that, regardless of the details, your primary in-struction from your Spirit, no matter the situation, will *always* be, "Radiate Love." As the highest frequency energy in our universe, and our assurance of being aligned with harmony, Love truly is the universal solution to all our problems.

JUST AS I DEMONSTRATED IN MY INITIAL SURRENDER EXPERIENCE, letting go of mental struggle and letting your Spirit realign everything for you is the path out of difficulty and upwards to Eden. The way up and out of the misaligned world is a simple matter of choosing the Love and divine wisdom of your Spirit over the influence of your myopic, fearful self. When you do that, you raise yourself to a vi-brational realm where the serpent cannot exist. When you are aligned with your Spirit, you starve the serpent in you of energy in reverse polarity, without which he can't survive. Remember: with every choice you make, you are either feeding "the angel" (God-In-You) or you are feeding the serpent. You are constantly choosing between empowering the schema for harmony or the schema for disharmony. Just choose harmony.

It's that simple, and henceforth, it will be *easier*, too. Believe me, I understand that staying awake and aware, being able to recognize who's who in the conversation in your mind, and overcoming your lower urges has probably not been that easy up till now. That is in large part because we've been going at it from the standpoint of *fighting* against the lower part of ourselves. When we fight something, we empower it by feeding it energy—and I'm sure I don't have to tell you what type of energy that *fighting* feeds off of! The way to disengage from the serpent is by rising above it to the vibrational level where it has no influence. Instead of spending energy resisting the lower aspects of you, you simply need to focus on aligning with your Spirit and rising up.

Fighting is hard. Loving your Spirit is easy. Loving your Spirit and radiating the Love that is generated by your Love response to your Spirit is really all you need to do to lift up out of the realm of the serpent. It couldn't be easier!

In this civilization, where we have for so long been aligned with the schema for disharmony, and where the false notion that hard work is the only way to accomplish anything of value reigns supreme, it may be a challenge to realize that *hard work and struggle are not the least bit helpful in the restoration process!* In fact, they are antithetical to it. Hard work, struggle, and complication are the purview of the misaligned mind. They are the very nutrients it needs to thrive!

Ease is the M.O. of your Spirit—and of your existence when you allow yourself to be realigned with It. When your Spirit is in charge and you are doing as you are designed to do, not only do ease and joy prevail, you are automatically raised in frequency to the level of self-realization. "But," your complication-addicted mind may be saying, "isn't achieving Nirvana supposed to be hard? Isn't enlightenment *supposed* to take years and years of effort and extreme self-discipline?"

Perhaps the reason all the millions of people who have been diligently and sincerely working hard to attain enlightenment all these years aren't there yet is not because it is so difficult to achieve but because it is so easy!

RAISING YOUR FREQUENCY AND RECREATING EDEN does not require any specific technique, though there are certainly some spiritual practices that can add dimension to your relationship with your Spirit, and your Spirit may even guide you toward some of them. There are many facets of your Love relationship with your Spirit to explore. But basically, it all boils down to one simple activity: radiating Love. That aligns us instantly with our Spirits, and raises our frequency by drawing Love into us and through us. Radiating Love is something we all innately know how to do because the ability is hardwired into us.

I recognize, however, that your structure-loving mind would very much like to be provided with a specific technique for this—a plan of sorts. Since we do need to enlist this part of us in our restoration, I will share with you something simple I came up with to assist my own mind in repositioning itself: in letting go and letting God. Please feel free to use it or not as your own Spirit directs. This is a "decree"—a kind of powerful, affirmative expression of intent—that I use when I find myself in particular need of realignment and wanting to feel the exquisite rush of rising in frequency to the vibrational level of pure joy. I believe the power of using it is that my mind is *actively engaged* in aligning with my Spirit and turning up the frequency.

I use this decree—or some version of it—in all kinds of circumstances, but I love using it the most when I am in private and can be lying on my back—on the bed, the floor, or even in my favorite location, the swimming pool—so that I am feeling vulnerable, like the underdog submitting to the "big dog" (essentially what you are doing when you're releasing yourself to your Spirit!). I close my eyes and breathe out whatever tension I'm experiencing and allow my body to go soft, and my conscious mind to go into neutral for a second so it can be flipped around in service to Spirit. (When in reverse, your brain, like a car transmission, needs to first go into neutral before it can change directions.) Then I say the words (sometimes silently, sometimes aloud) and feel them as I say them:

I release myself to you, Spirit. I am completely yours. I relax and soften every fiber of my being to be re-patterned according to the divine blueprint you provide for me. I open every cell and molecule to receive the light of Love you pour forth to me. As I receive this immense Love from the Heart of God, I feel your Love for me and my love for You filling my heart to overflowing and radiating out to bless the world and return home to you.

As I inhale, I feel the Love flooding into my cells. As I fill with Love, I am aware of rising in frequency and my heart swelling with joy. I use my breath to increase the influx and the feeling, and I mentally encourage myself to let go more and more and allow the expansion of Love throughout my being. Oftentimes, I feel physically lifted, like I'm about to levitate! When I am filled to overflowing with Love, I feel it radiating from me like light from a high-wattage bulb. What ecstasy!

As much as I love doing what I just described to you, it is not practical to go off apart from the rest of the world, lie down, and close your eyes on a full-time basis—you would miss out on doing the other activities your Spirit has for you to do! The goal is not to radiate Love only when it is convenient to have privacy and relax in the prone position, but to do it constantly and naturally, just as we were designed to do. So while making a special time to do it can be a powerful way to get in touch with how it feels to be properly aligned, filling up with Love, experiencing the Love-response to Spirit, and radiating it out, the goal is not to ritualize it, but to get to the point where you do it spontaneously without needing to make a special event of it.

It is helpful to frequently remind yourself to let go, and to deliberately feel Love radiating from you, until it becomes your modus operandi and you no longer have to initiate it consciously. In the meantime, whenever you feel yourself in need of realignment, or whenever you become aware of the serpent calling you downward in frequency, an effective response is to deliberately surrender to your Spirit instead.

Just as your conscious mind, during your Earth indoctrination, learned the dangerous operating procedure of aligning with the schema for disharmony by heeding the call of the serpent to misalignment, and allowing your intellect to run your life without input from Spirit, it can now take on the new habit of being aligned with your Spirit and with the Creator's Design for Harmony and Wholeness so that you can do your primary job as a human. It certainly has powerful motivation to—among other things, it now knows it is the only way to rise up out of the lower-vibrational world of pain and suffering!

In fact, because it is how you were designed to operate, it isn't really even a new pattern. Your mind will simply be defaulting to its original way of operating—its "factory-installed" setting! I can promise you that operating the way you were designed to is much, *much* easier than operating in opposition to it! And, speaking of your "fresh from the factory" condition, the next chapter is all about that.

CHAPTER SIX

Your Self:
Guardian of the Gate

*T*HE OPPORTUNITY BEFORE YOU IS TO TRANSFORM YOURSELF INTO A FRESH, NEW, LIGHT-FILLED BEING—a being that is as closely aligned with your Spirit as it is possible to be. You have been that before in this lifetime, whether you remember it or not, and you are headed toward being that again. You are becoming your *Self*. Your *true* Self. Your Self with a capital "S." When you become your Self once again, you will automatically find yourself in the Garden, because when you fully honor your divine blueprint, you will operate at the frequency of Paradise. After all, you were designed to dwell there.

The path to Paradise leads straight through your pure, unadulterated Self—the true You with nothing added—nothing added, that is, that does not enhance your ability to be who you truly are and to do what you are meant to do here on Planet Earth. This self that you are becoming is the *reclaimed version* of your Original Self, the pristine being you were before the dysfunctional patterns present on Planet Earth began to put their mark on you. *Your Original Self*

was perfectly aligned with your Spirit and operated at the highest fre-
quency possible for a human being. Your Original Self was basically
your Spirit with an Earth suit on, some special settings, tools, and
programming to help you play your particular role as a human
being, and that's about it!

This original version of you, with the right guidance and nurturing, could have matured into a grand adult being of immense
power and Light, but as we discussed in chapter 1, that was not to
be—at least not directly. The path to that was circumvented by
some pretty wide detours, but it is still to be your path.

While you have gathered many experiences in your life—some
life-enhancing, many not—and have picked up all kinds of programming and wounding that now manifests as someone who only
vaguely resembles your Original Self, your Original Self still remains. Though its light has been dimmed by being covered over by
the many vibration-lowering concepts, practices, and external influences you have become subject to since you were born, under-
neath, it is still intact. Like a high-wattage lamp that has layer after
layer of dirty rags obscuring its brilliant light from view, your Original Self is still burning brightly, too.

Your Original Self is your very essence and must be uncovered
so it can shine forth to illuminate the world again. Uncovering it is
not a project, however, and cannot be accomplished by working
hard to rid yourself of those "dirty rags." Instead, it is once again a
matter of performing the only transformational act necessary in
your return to Eden, and by now, I'm sure you know what that is!
Yes, becoming your Self is a simple matter of realigning yourself
with your Spirit, and allowing the parts of you that aren't a frequency match to be pulled vibrationally upward and spontaneously
transformed so that you can enter the Garden.

Your Self is the Gatekeeper of the Garden. As I stated in an
earlier chapter, Paradise has a built-in security system. *Only those*
who are operating at a high enough frequency can enter there. To enter, you must return to the vibrational level you most likely last
inhabited as an innocent, *un-adulterated* child. (I just love that term,
"unadulterated"—it sums up the concept so perfectly. To become
pure again, all that frequency-lowering stuff you picked up on the

way to becoming an adult must be released so that you return to the pristine, high-frequency child-state!)

It is truly an ingenious setup. The Garden cannot be entered by those who would foul it with energy in reverse polarity. It cannot be sullied by lower-vibrational muck, because until one reaches a certain vibrational level, Paradise simply *does not exist!* The higher-vibrational state one must be in to access the Garden cannot be manifested unless one is pure of heart and mind like a newborn child. Once there, one can only remain there to the extent that the lower-vibrational world is left behind. If one is seduced by lower-frequency thoughts as Adam and Eve were—and as I, myself, was during my Swiss mountaintop experience, one is "ejected" from the Garden—or more accurately, one is just not there anymore. The built-in security system described in the *Holy Bible* is responsible for this phenomenon.

In the *Bible* at the end of chapter 3 in the Book of Genesis, just after Adam and Eve are exiled from the Garden, it states "God stationed the *cherubim* and the flaming sword which turned every direction to guard the way to the tree of life."[1] In the generally accepted angelic hierarchy, the cherubim are second only to the seraphim, who reside next to God Himself.

In the way the *vibrational hierarchy* has been presented to me while writing this book, and as I have presented it, in turn, to you, I would compare "God Himself" to Source, the Core of Creation; the seraphim to your Spirit (God-In-You); and the cherubim to your Original Self, the pure, high-frequency being you were when you were first born. Cherubs are childlike angels, embodying the perfect innocence and balance of your original state. Flames, as in the "flaming swords," represent high frequency, the high frequency required to enter Eden's gate. It seems clear to me that what this passage in Genesis is saying is that you must return to the high-frequency state of an innocent child—the vibrationally pure being you were before you became polarized to the schema for disharmony—in order to enter the Garden.

The master teacher, Jesus, taught this very truth. "Truly, I say

---

1 *New American Standard Bible.*

to you, unless you turn and become like children, you will never enter the kingdom of heaven,"[2] he admonished his followers.

I believe he meant it literally—until you *turn* (*turn* away from the seduction of the world of energy in reverse polarity, allowing your receptivity to be fully to your Spirit) and become like a little child (with the high-vibrational purity of the child you were before Earth-life began to influence you) you can't get into the kingdom of heaven. I believe that Jesus was saying you have to raise your frequency up to the level it was when you first arrived here—to that of your Original Self—in order to live in a paradisiacal state again. Basically, the cherubim guarding the gate is *you*—the *true* you—and, until you become that again, you are locked out.

CAN YOU CONCEIVE OF YOUR ORIGINAL SELF? I mean really get in touch with what and who you were before Earth-life began to change you? What happens when you divest yourself of all your perceptions, experiences, feelings, preferences, relationships, behavioral patterning, learning, history, belongings, etcetera? What is left? Take a moment now to attune with this—to imagine yourself as if you had no history, no imprinting, no attachments. Can you get in touch with this "you"? Can you feel what that's like?

The first time I considered this question, it so completely blew me away, I had the same sensation as when I seriously contemplate the origin of Creation—you know, the "who created the Creator?" question that goes on into infinity—the one that always makes me lose my grip on reality (or the *consensus reality*, anyway). I'm pretty sure you know the feeling—it's like the sensation you have when you are going to sleep and suddenly feel you are falling out of bed, and awaken with a start. It's an ungrounded feeling—a feeling of being untethered.

That's what getting in touch with your Original Self, your essential being, may feel like to you, too. Without all that stuff weighing you down and tying you to your familiar world, it may feel like *you*

---

2 Matthew 18:3, *New American Standard Bible,* English Standard Version.

do not exist! We are so used to carrying the vibrational weight of our experiences, attachments, wounds, and all the rest, and so used to thinking—and mistakenly so—that all those things are *us*, it is strange to get in touch with who we would be without them. It is a lightness that you may find unsettling at first.

And yet, if you allow yourself to go with it—to release all of your baggage long enough to really get in touch with that pure you—you find someone remarkable: your Spirit in human form. This amazing being, this Spirit with a human body on, is your Original Self. It is the optimal version of you in *potential*. It is how you were in the beginning when you were still dwelling in the Garden, before the forbidden fruit was presented to you, before you took that initial bite.

This first and most pure version of the human you is to be your inspiration and beacon on your journey back to bliss. Of course, you can't actually be that exact being again—the one with no history on Earth—and you won't likely want to leave all your valuable learning and happy memories behind. It's not that you need to disown your experiences or forget that they happened, you simply need to transform the energy of them so that they do not vibrationally weigh you down. Just as you can't un-spill your milk, you can't un-live the history you've lived up till now, but what you can do is attune with your Spirit and allow your Spirit to draw you closer and closer until those adulterated parts of you are transformed and made like new again. The joyous parts are already of high frequency so those will remain; only the parts that are less than joyous will "go away."

I realize that the task at hand may seem huge and impossible. To go from where you are now, with all your attachments, biases, habits, emotional patterning, and mental programming, to a revised version of yourself that is clear enough and high enough in frequency to access the Garden must seem like an overwhelming undertaking. But I know from my own experience that it is not. Yes, it is impossible if you think you have to do it utilizing the ordinary means of working hard to change yourself—in that sense, it really *is* impossible. But from the standpoint of releasing yourself—and the process—to your Spirit, it is not only possible, it is your destiny. And it is easy! Prime Principle—and specifically, the power of unified radiance—makes this truly do-able.

As you draw closer to merging with your Spirit, and more and more of you is transformed as a result, all the pertinent data, memories, and programming stored in your brain; all the energy patternings that are in alignment with your Spirit and with your true purpose for being, will remain, and, indeed, become more focused in your consciousness. Those aspects that don't support your true purpose will simply cease to exist. As you allow this to happen, you will become your Self, shining like new again.

WE'VE CONSIDERED THE CONCEPT OF THE "PURE YOU" WITH NOTHING ADDED— your Original Self, your essence. Now, let's imagine who you would be if you had grown up in the idealized, healthy world with the idealized, healthy caretakers we have visualized earlier. Can you dare imagine the person you might be now? When I imagine my "Possible Self," I envision a powerful and fearless, self-confident, fully expressive, unconditionally loving, passionate, effective, effervescent woman, sizzling with energy, who stays in the moment and is open-minded, totally creative, balanced physically, mentally/ emotionally, and spiritually; who is constantly attuned with and following her Spirit without hesitation; who enjoys every moment of her life—and whose very existence greatly enhances the Whole of Creation. I envision my Spirit expressing as me.

To paint your own picture of who and what you would be, you might try making a list of the qualities that constitute what a fully radiant human being would be. For starters, you might ask yourself, "What qualities do I most admire in myself? What qualities do I most admire in others?" Then use these to paint a picture in your mind of who you would be if you could claim all those qualities for yourself, with nothing undesirable added in. And then "supercharge" your vision of this Self with the idea of being more radiant, more vital, and capable of more amazing feats than any human being you've ever encountered!

This exercise will give you a vague notion of the grandeur you were designed to embody. It will also provide a list of qualities that you embodied before your time on Earth decommissioned them. Yes, I am betting you possessed all of your most admired qualities when you were a young child—or at least you did before your Earth indoctrination modified you. We all did.

The qualities that make people vital, dynamic, attractive, and effective in the world are those that enable Life Force to channel through them and to radiate from them. These are the very qualities you need to claim for yourself—indeed, *re-claim*—if you are to do your job here. If this seems impossible based on your years of trying to "improve" yourself with limited success, worry not. This is a whole new approach. Becoming your Self is not a matter of taking on characteristics that are foreign to you but a matter of letting the parts of you that you shut down in response to the harsh conditions of your Earth indoctrination be restored by the power of your Spirit.

TO UNDERSTAND THE IMPORTANCE OF THESE QUALITIES, of these tools, it will be helpful to understand the basic purpose for which they were installed in you. They are for effectively maintaining your alignment and for managing the energy flow through you, as well as for utilizing that energy to prosper the Whole. You see, while perfect alignment with Source is the most critical aspect of raising and keeping your frequency high, there is another part of the equation that is highly important as well: efficient, effective energy management.

If you are to utilize the Life Force from Source to do the job for which you were created, you must be able to not only receive energy, but dynamically channel the energy you receive, and before it radiates from you, your energy must be able to circulate freely through you. You can't raise or keep your frequency high without continually moving energy in and through you. Basically, as a receiver and transmitter of Love, moving energy is your job!

Just as a blocked plumbing pipe prevents water from flowing freely through, your body-mind cannot fully move energy if there are blockages to the flow. This is really important because your frequency level—and thus, your proximity to Paradise—depends on the movement of energy through you. Sadly, as we discussed in chapter 1, there have been many influences that have caused you to stop the free movement of energy through you, damming up and storing now-stagnant energy which continues to impede the free-flow of Love/Life Force through you, energy necessary for optimal health. Happily, once you realign yourself with your Spirit and intend to radiate that mighty flow of Love, these blockages can be dissolved more easily than you think.

If you have already spent time trying to remove blocks to your energy flow in your physical, emotional, or mental aspects, you may have a preconceived notion about how difficult that is. I ask you to suspend these ideas based on past experience. You will not be approaching this task from the level of the blockage. Instead, you will be recommissioning your energy-moving qualities, thus raising your frequency and engaging Prime Principle so that, by the power of unified radiance, the blockages will clear spontaneously!

WHEN YOU FIRST MADE YOUR DEBUT HERE ON PLANET EARTH, you were fully equipped with all the tools—all the qualities, the characteristics—you would need to keep you vital and connected, receiving and circulating optimal levels of Life Force so that you could do your job as an interface between Spirit and the physical world. You came with everything you would need to be an effective radiator of Love. These tools were integral to your design and still are. To keep them in sound working order, however, they needed to have been fully utilized. Sadly, conditions here on Earth not only did not support the full use of these tools, they contributed to your lack of understanding and appreciation of them.

I really want to emphasize that there is absolutely nothing in your design that is incidental, accidental, or otherwise nonessential. There may be parts of us that have become out of balance to an absurd proportion, and there may be aspects of our design that we don't understand or that we have forgotten the purposes and importance of, but there is nothing about our design—or the design of the Whole of Creation, for that matter—that isn't crucial to the proper workings of it.

It would seem, however, that we humans have taken many of our most important characteristics for granted, and virtually quit using others. We've even allowed them to be hijacked by reverse-polarity aspects of ourselves to serve lower-frequency agendas instead of for serving Spirit as they were designed. If we are going to revitalize ourselves so that we can do what we came here for, and recreate a sustainable Heaven on Earth, we will need to reclaim them for our Spirits and make fully utilizing them—in balanced, healthy ways—a high priority.

So what are these qualities I've dubbed your "Qualities of Origin?" What are these important tools and settings that our Original Selves came equipped with? These powerful energy-management devices are: Unconditional Acceptance, Ease Orientation, Emotional Expressiveness, Physical Expressiveness, Present-time Orientation, Impeccable Honesty, Open-heartedness, Open-mindedness, Vocal Expressiveness, Complete Creativity, Possibility Thinking, Imagination, Playfulness, Faith, Wholeheartedness, Energy Balance, and Joyfulness.

Remember, these are all qualities possessed by your Original Self, *qualities that are characteristic of beings who reside in Paradise.* Thus, they must be reclaimed to access that sublime state and truly be your Self. By reclaiming them in their fullness, and exercising them in the way that you were designed to, you unblock the impedances to the free flow of energy through you and, thus, raise your frequency. While it would take an entire book to do justice to these tools—and such a book is likely forthcoming—for now I will at least hit the highlights of many of them here so that you will better understand their importance and can begin to think in terms of reclaiming your full use of them. To that purpose, here are some brief descriptions:

- *Unconditional Acceptance.* Unconditional Acceptance is a most powerful quality. You were born accepting everything without qualification. You accepted your body, your mother's love, your drunken uncle, the shack or mansion you lived in—even your feces—*without judgment*. (Remember judgment? The very stance that shifts you out of the Garden?) Granted, some of the things I named were not necessarily in harmony with the Whole, and you may certainly have liked some things more than others, but you *did not judge*. Until you were taught to do so, you made no judgments about anything! Remember: in the Garden (where you were dwelling in consciousness at that time—or at least in the close proximity of it), nothing is good or evil, right or wrong—it simply *is*. Unconditional acceptance does not mean you condone something; it merely means you acknowledge it without judgment. And if you believe something needs to change, it's still necessary to accept how it is first. Acceptance is the point at which true change can occur, as only when you are in alignment—in nonjudgment—can you marshal the Love that is necessary to transform anything.

- *Ease Orientation.* Ease Orientation is certainly one of the more misunderstood Qualities of Origin. Somehow we have internalized a false belief that things need to be difficult to be authentic, and that if it comes easily, it is not worth much. Nothing could be further from the truth! *Ease* is a hallmark of Paradise and the Divine Design for Wholeness. Of course, ease at the expense of others is not true ease. The ease I am speaking of is the ease that is the result of allowing your Spirit to orchestrate events and your actions so as to be in harmony. In this context, when things are easy, it means you are aligned with the schema for harmony. Ease is an indicator that you are in the flow. In the Garden, everything is easy. In the misaligned world, things are hard. If something you undertake is difficult, it is an indicator that you are not fully surrendered to your Spirit and are aligned with the schema for disharmony, instead of with the Creator's Design for Harmony and Wholeness. While the schema for disharmony still has a strong grip in the consensus reality, being aligned with your Spirit for greater ease is not just a convenience issue; it's a matter of life and death!

- *Emotional Expressiveness.* One of the greatest energy-expediting tools we fully utilize as infants is Emotional Expressiveness. When we feel happy, we coo with contentment. When we feel a great current of Love sweep over us, we fling our arms around the nearest dear one and proclaim our love. When we feel angry, we don't hesitate to discharge the out-of-harmony energy that caused it. Your emotions are energy-monitoring tools that indicate when energy is in harmony or out of it. As young ones, when we come into contact with energy out of harmony, we do not hold back—we howl in pain and the tears flow! One of the great tragedies of our training to fit in to the dysfunctional world is that we are taught to disown our emotions, or at the least, to keep them to ourselves and stop the energy that activated them from moving through and out of us. By stuffing down and damming up these strong energies, we create serious blockages that manifest in everything from deep resentments and unsuccessful relationships, to murderous, out-of-control energy, and fatal disease in our bodies. One of your greatest opportunities in reclaiming your Original Self is in learning how to express your emotions freely in healthy ways in the moment to keep energy moving freely through you. And, as you will discover, keeping your emotional body free and clear greatly enhances your ability to be proactively joyful!

- *Physical Expressiveness.* Physical Expressiveness is trained out of us to a greater or lesser degree early on. "Sit down and be still" is one of the most often-employed commands given by parents to children who are simply moving in response to the powerful energy flowing through them. Your body is a kinetic masterpiece. It is designed to MOVE, and when it does not, it suffers greatly. Remember how it was when so much energy was coursing through you that you were in almost perpetual motion—running, jumping, twirling, dancing—and you were not at all self-conscious about the way you moved your body? Put on some lively music for a group of children, and they spontaneously begin to dance, allowing their bodies to freely respond to the music. Do this with a group of adults—even *encourage*

105

them to dance—and watch how self-consciously they move, if at all! Of course, much of this is due to the fear of what others will think, which is just a version of ignoring the voice of Spirit within in deference to external authority—the almighty opinion of others. To be healthy and free, and move energy in the way you were intended to, you need to be able to respond freely to the movement of energy in and through you, channeling it in constructive ways.

- *Present-time Orientation.* You were always in the "now" when you were a Planet Earth "newbie." When you are born on Earth, you are a timeless being, coming from a timeless dimension, entering a zone where the mental construct of linear time is in play. As such, you had no concept of time as a baby and were not aware of the future or past. These are mental concepts, generated by duality, that create fragmentation of your attention and focus, thus diminishing your ability to interact with the dynamic flow of Life Force. In order to steward energy, your mind must be available to it—it must be where the energy is—something it cannot be when you are focused into the past or future. Being focused in the *now* is a mental setting that allows you to have full, authentic, effective, and, yes, *satisfying* experiences of interacting with the flow of Life Force. Because energy exists only in the *now*, keeping your attention focused in the present moment is key to being accurately attuned with the current configuration and timely movement of the Whole for optimal coordination with it. As challenging as it is in a linear-time culture to stay in the now, Present-time Orientation is a positioning in consciousness that is absolutely vital.

- *Impeccable Honesty.* Impeccable Honesty positions you relative to the flow of Life Force such that you are completely energized; being dishonest removes you from the direct flow of Life Force. Being honest—or not—is at essence not a moral issue but an energy issue. When you are dishonest, you are disowning your response-ability for the energy you have drawn to you and you are stepping out of the flow of Life Force. When you are a child, you are completely honest and deceit never enters your modus operandi until you observe it in others, or until someone encourages you to be less than honest to either save yourself from having to take responsibility for something you did, or to preserve someone's ego. We begin to perceive dishonesty as a survival tool and learn to use it to dodge uncomfortable situations (often in the attempt to escape the consequences of violating Prime Principle). In reality, what we are doing is aligning with energy in reverse polarity and, hence, taking ourselves out of the flow of Life Force—which is certainly *not* a survival tool! Being impeccably honest, no matter the perceived risk, and trusting our Spirits to guide us through keeps us in the only place of power and in the only place of true safety—properly aligned to receive the flow of Life Force from Source and aligned with energy in harmony.

- *Open-heartedness.* When you are born, your heart is wide open, ready to give Love and receive Love freely and without reservation, just as does the Heart of God. But as inharmonious energy begins to process through the emotional body causing pain, you learn to shut down your heart in an attempt to lessen the pain. Of course, Love is never hurtful, but when you shut down your heart center, you diminish your ability to give and receive Love. Open-heartedness is the willingness to remain open to the movement of energy through your heart center. Based on Prime Principle and the laws of attraction, consistent radiation of Love from your heart is the only thing that can truly protect your heart, so shutting down may dull the pain, but it also diminishes the flow of Love. Since Love is the only transformational force, shutting down in the face of misaligned energy is a failure to do the only thing that can transform misaligned energy. Because your primary function as a human on Earth is to radiate the Love that emanates from Source, thus restoring misaligned energy to harmony by the power of unified radiance, restoring Open-heartedness is of primary importance to doing what you were designed to do. Transforming energy through your open-hearted giving and receiving of Love is required for bringing your world up in frequency for the recreation of Eden.

- *Open-mindedness.* In addition to keeping an open heart, Open-mindedness is another prime quality to be maintained in returning to a paradisiacal state. I say "maintained" instead of "reclaimed" because I doubt if you'd have read this far if you weren't open-minded! When you were born, your mind was totally open and available to whatever stimulation and information was presented to it. But instead of being taught of the limitless possibilities of the vast Universe, you were taught "the way things are" on Earth and you probably learned, at least in part, to close your mind to ideas and energies that did not fit into the conceptual reality that prevailed, and in time, to ideas that didn't fit with your own already-established concepts. Being open-minded means maintaining mental flexibility. It means having a willingness to consider new or expanded ideas, letting your Spirit guide you in sorting out the ones in which to invest Life Force, and the ones to discard. It means having the willingness to let Life Force forge new creative pathways in your brain. Open-mindedness is a great evolutionary advantage in a universe whose very nature is change! In order to be able to create a new and more harmonious reality, we need to be willing to accommodate new energies and new ideas.

- *Vocal Expressiveness.* Vocal Expressiveness is one of your most potent energy tools. Your voice is designed to provide more than a way to communicate and make music—it is an energy balancing, moving, transferring, and linking instrument. It is thought by some that in the ancient past, humans used their voices to raise frequency and set up energy waves capable of altering matter and manifesting material things. These days, such knowledge is obscure and the power of the human voice is undervalued. Its uses beyond being a tool for verbal communication and as a musical instrument have largely been forgotten, which is tragic considering it is one of our most valuable energy-raising implements. In the beginning of our Earth sojourn, we are totally vocally expressive but are quickly launched on a program of vocal repression. As children, we are conditioned to "bite our tongues" rather than to speak out and express our thoughts and feelings, thus we initiate the pattern of holding this energy inside, causing chronic blockages of Life Force. When we sing— something we do spontaneously as young children—we may be compared to others and made to feel self-conscious about it. We are also admonished by adults to stop "making noise just to make it," even when the sounds we are making are, in truth, often our innate wisdom using our voices to balance us or release trapped energy. Reclaiming the free and easy use of your voice and honoring it and putting it into service as a frequency-raising, energy-balancing, and energy-expediting tool can take you far— and fast—up the Garden path.

- *Complete Creativity.* We are created in the image and likeness of The Creator. Therefore, we were born with the quality of Complete Creativity installed as our premier tool. And oh, how creative we were created to be! Because your very nature is to create, you are always creating, whether consciously or unconsciously, with the Life Force flowing through you manifesting your reality according to the patterns present in your mind. Whether you are ready to own this or not, you have created everything in your world—and continue to create—with the cooperation of universal forces, either on purpose or by default. The problem with many of your creations is that they were manifested from seeds that came from the reverse-polarity world. Anything manifested without the direct inspiration of Spirit is bound to be flawed. A major step in becoming who you were designed to be is owning your creations, assuming responsibility for your creative capacity, and using only seeds from your Spirit to create from. Turning over your life to your Spirit, receiving your Spirit's divine input, and letting your Spirit transform your mind so that what you create is of increasingly higher vibration and greater harmony is obviously key in creating the higher-vibrational state of being we know as Paradise.

- *Possibility Thinking.* The creative process involves *all* the Qualities of Origin, and, as a creator, you come equipped with many specialized tools that support your creativity. One of them is Possibility Thinking. As children, we had no concept of limitations. We were "possibility thinkers" who assumed, and rightly so, that whatever we could think of or imagine, we could create and experience. And as a part of the Great Mind of God, we can! We've simply been convinced, by our own evidence-loving, limitation-loving minds, to think we can't—and thus, in effect, we can't. Remember, because of his alignment with reverse polarity, the Adam in you isn't directly connected to the realm of all possibilities. He can only see that which has already been created out in the misaligned world, so he basically believes that what is already in existence, flawed though it may be—or variations thereof—is all that is possible. (Fortunately, revolutionary ideas manage to slip into our psyches while Adam is snoozing!) Nothing is created without the belief—at some level—that it is possible, and *so* much more is possible than most people believe. If we are to expand the scope of our creativity and the bounds of our reality, we must release our false belief in limitation and embrace possibility thinking once more. *Paradise depends on it.*

- *Imagination.* Imagination is the part of you that your Spirit communicates through and is the crown jewel of your creativity tool kit. Your imagination is the staging area for ideas from your Spirit to be pulled down by Eve and translated into form by Adam. Your imagination provides the seeds from which all manifestation takes place, and is what creates the template for Life Force to flow into in the creative process. When we first arrive on the planet, our imaginations are unbounded, and we are able to tap into higher realms of energy and easily retrieve ideas from there. But because our Possibility Thinking is discouraged, we also are discouraged from believing that which we imagine is anything more than fancy, especially when it doesn't match what the consensus reality says is possible. And so, all too often, we abandon truly imaginative thinking in favor

of that which fits with the mainstream. All the great art, litera-
ture, inventions, and technological advances in human history
have been due to possibility-thinkers who refused to contain
their thinking to "inside the box" (the box that the logical mind
maintains due to its limited view). Instead, they aligned themselves to reach upward in frequency into their imaginations to
retrieve ideas from the Great Mind of God via their Spirits.

- *Playfulness.* Playfulness and imagination go hand in hand—imagination provides the creative seeds, and play holds these seeds
at a vibrational level where manifestation can easily take place.
Playfulness is another potent creativity tool you had in abundance as a new Earthling. As children, our capacity for play is
seemingly inexhaustible, but as we are conditioned to the civilization in which we are to spend our lives, we are taught that
play (and later, what *passes* for play in the adult world) is for
certain prescribed times only. This is unfortunate because true
unadulterated play lifts and keeps your vibrations high, positioning you to receive a greater flow of Life Force. It's no wonder we feel so good when we immerse ourselves in true play—
it brings us up into the realm of our Spirits! Playfulness lifts,
lightens, and breaks up energy patterns, making energy available to flow into new forms, and frees it for alignment with the
Whole. It frees *you* to align with the Whole! Play is a powerful
creative tool that not only helps you manifest your desires, but
speeds up the trip back to the Garden—and makes it a lot of fun!

- *Faith.* Faith is yet another vital piece of your creative equipment. What you have complete faith in *will* come to pass, and
you are always having faith in something—often, in exactly what
you *don't* want to happen! *Rightly applied,* however, faith is a
technology that creates a bridge between what is, and what you
desire (which, if it is inspired by your Spirit, is always the highest of possibilities). Faith is a knowing, without external confir-
mation, that, as long as it is not in opposition to your Spirit's
intentions, what you have faith in is manifesting as a reality for
you. Faith is the vital tool that *sustains* energy when external

evidence is unavailable (clearly something that Eve is more comfortable with than is Adam), and connects your "now" energy with the form of your highest possible future. When you arrived on Earth, you had complete and utter faith—it is one of your "factory-installed" tools for creating—but as you became more and more immersed in the concepts of a civilization that long ago mistook its own misalignment with a fault in God's perfect system, you may have abandoned utilizing faith as a method for aligning more closely with the Divine Design and creating harmoniously. It is time to reclaim it! Faith is, perhaps, your most powerful tool in recreating Paradise, as when you have it, all else arranges itself "magically" to bring that in which you have faith to manifestation.

- *Wholeheartedness.* Wholeheartedness is another major tool in your creativity kit. As children, we are naturally enthusiastic and passionate about all kinds of things, throwing ourselves *wholeheartedly* into that which we are moved to do. As we are directed by external authority to do things for which we have no energy or interest (energy and interest are powerful signs pointing toward that which we are meant to be doing), our ability to put our hearts—our emotions—into what we're doing is hampered. Since our emotions are the fuel for our creations, it is critical that our hearts are in that which we do. Indeed, your heart and your Spirit have a special connection. Your heart center is not only the seat of your emotional body, which monitors energy for integrity (and always finds your Spirit's energy to be of the highest caliber, of course!), it is the part of you that has always stayed most closely attuned with your Spirit due to its role in the Love response. Know that whatever is true to your heart is true to your Spirit's patterning and worthy of your passion. *Reclaiming your authority to decide what to pour your passion into* is the key to restoring the powerful tool of wholeheartedness so that energy can be freed up and directed fully into those things that are consonant with your Spirit, aligned with your purpose, and fully in harmony with the Whole. Those are the very things you will naturally put your "whole heart"

YOUR SELF: GUARDIAN OF THE GATE

into, and thus, they will be of the highest integrity and of greatest value to you and the planet.

- *Energy Balance.* Energy Balance is one of your default settings as a new resident of Earth. It is a quality that rightly would govern all other qualities, as it is a state that needs to be maintained at all times in every process and every aspect of you for wholeness and optimum vitality. When you are born, energy comes in and energy moves out in equal measure. Whether it be that you take in a certain amount of calories and immediately expend those calories in movement and metabolism, or whether it be that an idea comes into your consciousness and you immediately act upon it, your outflow is commensurate with your inflow. Over time as we become aligned with the imbalanced energy patterns on Earth, our own energy patterns become unbalanced as well. Rebalancing our energy flow in all aspects is important in restoring ourselves to Paradise. Rebalancing our energy flow, as you may have deduced, is dependent upon getting Adam and Eve working together again so that Love issuing from Source is received and utilized efficiently as it was designed to be.

- *Joyfulness.* Another of your default settings is Joyfulness. As we discussed before, the hallmark of the realm of your Spirit is joy, and you are as close to your Spirit vibrationally when you are born as you ever are again (until you become your Self, that is). When you are residing in the upper levels of frequency as you are when you are a new Earthling, before you begin your descent into chronic misalignment and become affected by energy in reverse polarity, you are naturally, perpetually joyful! Instead of joyfulness being a rare state, it is your foundational state of being. Somewhere along the line, however, you begin to dwell at a lower frequency, and that becomes your normal vibrational home, with the joy-space becoming an infrequently visited vacation home. To restore your life to the vibrational state that is the location of Paradise, you will need to reclaim joy as your natural setting. This comes easily as you surrender more and more of yourself to your Spirit. True joy is a high-frequency phenomenon. While you can get "juice" from a rush of energy in reverse polarity, such as you might experience when, say, a sports team you don't like loses a big game, or when you hear that someone you think wronged you "got his," *actual* joy is not a response to outer stimuli, or a reverse-polarity phenomenon. Joy is not the same as something that excites or edifies your ego-self; it is an emotional response to the Love pouring forth from your Spirit into your heart center. Joy is a signpost on the path back to Eden—when you experience it, you know you are headed in the right direction. When you can sustain it, you know you are back in Eden.

Are you surprised at the simplicity of these? Are you appreciating these qualities in a way you never have before? Do you, like me, feel sadness—even a bit of resentment—at your forced abandonment or disowning of the very characteristics provided by your creator to maintain your health, your vitality, and your power in the world, not to mention your key to the Garden gate? Have you, too, begun to glimpse the awesome power in merely utilizing in a greater way these qualities that were built into your very nature? Years ago, when I gave a presentation on these qualities to a gathering of a couple of dozen men and women, after my descriptions of them and their purposes, a majority of the group (not just the women, either!) were in tears from the recognition of what they had lost. These qualities are your treasures and it is time to reclaim them.

Learning to fully express your Qualities of Origin is critical in raising your frequency, becoming your Self, and doing your primary job as a radiator of Love. Please let me reassure you that whereas it may look like a long road from where you are now to the point where you are fully utilizing these qualities, it is not the overwhelming, impossible task it would be if you had to approach it in the old way of blood, sweat, and tears.

To reclaim these innate qualities, all that is necessary is your *intention*, your attention, and most of all, your proper alignment with your Spirit. Being aware of the necessity of reclaiming them is a huge first step. Trusting that you will be guided and empowered by your Spirit in the process is really all the action you need to take for now. When you surrender to the process of allowing your Spirit to steward your life, these characteristics will spontaneously begin to strengthen in you, and you will be guided as needed in remembering how to utilize these tools for doing your job as a radiator of Love.

YOUR MISSION, THEN, IS TO BECOME THE EVOLVED YOU—the you that has come full circle back to high frequency. You are to unify with your Spirit once again and become your Self, utilizing all the energy tools you were provided to do your job as a radiator of Love. In the process, you are to shed whatever has kept your Spirit from being fully able to express through you, as you. Once you do, the gate to the Garden will open automatically. The gatekeeper to the Garden is your Self.

CHAPTER SEVEN

Recreating Eden:
The Time Is Now!

*I*F YOU HAVE EVER ASKED THE QUESTION, "WHY AM I HERE?" then you now
have your answer. You are here to recreate Heaven on Earth by
becoming your Self. You become your Self by surrendering to the
dominion of your Spirit—God-In-You—and loving your Spirit completely. In so doing, you raise yourself up in frequency so that you
are seamlessly aligned and vibrationally merged with this highest
level of your being, thus becoming the perfect expression of your
Spirit in human form, radiating Love to bless all of Creation.

As this occurs, it creates an effect so powerful, everything in
your world is utterly transformed and Eden manifests in your experience. Even before you reach the vibrational level of Eden, you
will experience improvements in your life that you can hardly even
fathom from where you are now! As you raise your own frequency
upward toward Eden, the frequency of the Whole of Creation is
raised as well and brings all within it closer to Eden, too. When
enough of us reach the vibrational level where Eden is our reality,

this paradisiacal state of being will begin to rapidly manifest as a widespread phenomenon—not just for the relative few that have chosen to lead the way—but, in time, for all.

Indeed, that is why you are here on Earth at this particular moment. I know this about you because, unless you are my relative, friend, or a book reviewer, you would not have been attracted to this book and read this far if you were not! I submit that you are here on the planet now because you have *chosen* to be. You have chosen to participate in the restoration of humanity to the Garden. If you have wished to be "one of the Chosen Ones," I can assure you that you are. You chose yourself . . . or rather, your Self.

Many—perhaps even you—have thought that the "Chosen Ones" meant those who were going to be tapped to physically escape Earth and be whisked away to some faraway heaven where they would not be touched by energy in reverse polarity. This is a gross misunderstanding. While you will, indeed, escape the travails of Earth and the ravages of the schema for disharmony, *abandoning* our beautiful planetary home is not what is intended at all. Rather, we "Chosen Ones" are to do the simple but vital things that are necessary to raise all of humanity up in frequency and create a new heavenly reality here, where energy in reverse polarity is not in control but where Love and harmony with the Whole of Creation are what we live by. And it is not to happen in some future time. It is to happen *now*.

If this sounds like a superhuman challenge, let me first assure you that as you rise in frequency, superhuman attributes are automatically yours—however, it will not take any superhuman effort from your personality-self at all. It will simply require that you let the divine, superhuman part of you steer your life so that you can align with the schema for harmony, thus empowering it in your own life and in the Whole of Creation. Because of the way the Divine Design works, the person you are *right now* is truly capable of this task no matter how daunting it may seem! As this chapter further unfolds, you will see just how this can be.

As I have written this, I have so many times asked the questions: "Is this *really* doable? Will this actually work—not just in theory but in reality? Will people really get on board with this, as ego-invested as most are in the current way things are on Planet Earth?" The answer that has come back over and over again is, "Absolutely!"

Why? We all have the memories of Paradise encoded in us. We all know, at least subconsciously, life on Earth is currently but a shadow of that—a dark shadow—and we all know that a radical change is needed but we just haven't understood the mechanics of what was wrong and how easily it could be changed. Not to mention, many—if not *most*—of us have reached our tolerance with the messed-up way things are! Restoring Earth to the Eden it was meant to be has looked like an impossible challenge—something only a band of saints could accomplish. After all, few of us are altruistic enough to make huge, personal sacrifices for the common good, however much we might like to be. Nor are most human beings induced to radical action by the unlikely seeming prospect of a big-picture concept like Utopia, however seductive a notion. If so, it would have been accomplished by now.

But altruism is not a requirement, nor is saintliness or sacrifice! The genius of this system of restoration is that it takes human nature fully into account, and inherent in it is all the motivation needed to get us on board with it. What could be more enticing than immediate life enhancement without hard work? Though human nature doesn't easily accommodate the giving up of what we personally treasure now for a distant dream of a better life for all, most of us can really get behind something that offers instant benefits for ourselves—something that offers relief from our miseries, and a far better life experience *now* and forevermore. Most of us can buy wholeheartedly into something effortless that pays out in vast *personal* riches—the true riches that will fill your yearnings like nothing else ever will.

That's the beauty of this process—you can't recreate Paradise on the planet without making your *own* experience of life one of exquisite joy and harmony. It can't be created from anywhere but within yourself. Only by improving your own life beyond measure will the larger story of Heaven on Earth unfold. When you take care of the "small picture," and do what is necessary to elevate yourself in frequency to the realm of joy, the Big Picture will take care of itself! And the only thing you will need to sacrifice is the behavior that got us into this mess—the tendency our ego-minds have to try to "run the show" without the stewardship of our Spirits. That is hardly a sacrifice, as will be evident as your life is brought into harmony by your Spirit!

This plan for restoration is so exquisitely simple, so remarkably easy, and so amazingly ingenious, you would almost think it was designed by the Highest Intelligence! (Please remember, this is not *my* plan. I'm just describing the Divine Design, in existence well before the first humans were ever created.) Not only is the restoration of Heaven to Earth a cinch to accomplish, the time has arrived for this plan to be implemented and for Eden to manifest once again. It's been a long, long time coming, but the time is *now*.

INDEED, THIS POINT IN HUMAN HISTORY IS UNPRECEDENTED. Many factors have at last lined up to make Paradise accessible to us once again, not the least of which is cosmic timing. In almost every spiritual tradition, there is mention of the larger cycles of Creation—the overriding succession of events that governs things from the highest levels to the most minute. One such concept, woven in one form or other throughout many spiritual teachings, is the idea that *God breathes in and out.*

Though these breaths are brief in the history of Creation, they encompass many thousands of years in human time. As God breathes out, Creation is expanded away from its core. When God breathes in, Creation contracts and is drawn back to the core. At this point in the cycles governing Creation, we have reached the end of the "out-breath" of God, and the "in-breath" has begun. Because of this, we are now, at last, able to more easily accomplish the return to Eden as the very in-breath of God is pulling us closer to the core of Creation and, thus, *higher in frequency.* Remember, the Garden exists at the highest frequency possible for human beings to experience, a frequency far higher than that at which we are currently operating.

It is also true that many, many humans have been working toward this—some knowingly, some not—for hundreds, for thousands of years. The substance they have generated in this regard and the holding of the line vibrationally, so to speak, have made it possible for us to be awake and aware of this now. If you think *you* have had a hard time overcoming spiritual inertia, be glad you aren't trying to achieve this in centuries past when God was still breathing out and the Whole of Creation had yet to be "turned around." Talk about a challenge! I have immense appreciation for those souls whose job it was to maintain spiritual awareness in the darkest of times before the conditions were optimal for humanity to head for Home.

Can you even imagine what it took for Jesus to incarnate on Earth over two millennia ago when human consciousness was hardly at its peak, and when expressing revolutionary ideas was likely to be fatal? Can you conceive of the immense Love he demonstrated by agreeing to leave his vibrational position close to the Core of Creation and lower his frequency sufficiently to reenter the schema for disharmony so that he could help us see the way up out of it? What amazing courage he displayed by subjecting himself to a reverse-polarity world experience of horrific pain, suffering, and death so that he could show us that it is possible to go from the depths of the schema for disharmony to the heights of Heaven by loving and obeying God with all our hearts and minds. And what amazing lessons he produced for us in showing the power of high frequency to heal when he touched the sick to make them well, and raised the dead with the mighty flow of Life Force he was channeling! And I can't leave out how he showed us the ultimate healing power of the Spirit when he resurrected his body by infusing his Spirit fully back into it before ascending once again. He called us to demonstrate the same "miracles" that he did—and when our frequency is at the necessary level, we will do as Jesus tapped us to do in a sort of passing of the baton: "Truly, truly, I say to you, he who believes in Me, the works that I do, he will do also; and greater works than these he will do; because I go to the Father."[1]

While there have been relatively few advanced souls whose sacrifices have been quite so visible as those of Jesus, there have been legions of "ordinary" folks whose job it has been to quietly

---

1 John 14:12, *New American Standard Bible.*

maintain spiritual awareness in the darkest of times before the conditions were optimal for humanity to head for Home. You may, indeed, have felt like this hard road was your lot, and I thank you from the bottom of my heart for holding steady and continuing to grow—and glow—in the dark. Those of us who have chosen to awaken prior to this current accelerated time have been catalysts for this process, and it hasn't always been fun. I asked Spirit once why I had to awaken and achieve my spiritual awareness amid so many people who were still asleep and who didn't honor my knowing or my process. I asked why I couldn't just go live in an ashram or a convent and "be spiritual" where I wouldn't feel so alone, misunderstood, and oppressed, and where it would be easier to consistently behave in concert with the level of consciousness I had attained. The answer that came was, "The yeast can't raise the bread unless it is mixed into the dough. It does no good for the yeast to float on top—it has to be *a part* of the dough if it is to lift it up."

And so it has been with you, too. That is why you have been experiencing the awakening process in the milieu of your every-day life, challenging though it has been. It is no accident that you find yourself in the midst of what may sometimes seem like an alien existence, surrounded by people who may not have a clue about what you are up to, much less share your perceptions. This is no accident or misfortune! Your Spirit has chosen to position you as you are because your increasing frequency is the leavening agent that raises up that which surrounds you.

Yes, in order for the yeast to be able to raise the bread, it must first grow and multiply and be incorporated into the dough. Once it is, it can create a loaf that is light as a feather in relatively short order. The happy news for humanity is that the yeast is finally developed, it is well mixed into the dough, and all the conditions are right for the loaf to rise.

WHEN I FOUND MYSELF BACK IN EDEN THAT AMAZING DAY at the top of the Zürichberg, I experienced such ecstasy I might never have left.

But though I couldn't have explained it at the time, I felt the consensus reality generated by so many minds operating out of alignment—the currents of energy in reverse polarity—tugging me back. So not only was my ego-mind eager to jump in and weigh and measure the experience and claim it for itself, thus pulling me back to the more familiar world of separation, it was as if the weight of the world was pulling me back as well. At first, I felt like a failure for not having been able to stay—for not having been able to prolong the experience of Oneness. As it turns out, this was not a failing at all. It just wasn't time yet.

I realize now that in addition to my ego-mind's powerful drive to stay separate, there simply was not enough vibrational support available in the world around me to assist me in staying at the lofty level I had attained. There was not yet sufficient human substance in conscious alignment—not only within me, personally, but within all of humanity—to make it easy for my ego to let go completely to the place in consciousness called "Oneness."

The currents of energy in reverse polarity were too strong, and I had not developed completely enough to maintain that state of being despite those reverse-polarity currents. What I needed—and what we have all needed—was for enough magnets to be aligned, both within what we consider "ourselves" and within the Whole of Creation, that we would be vibrationally buoyed up, not dragged down.

The point in the larger cycle of the Whole of Creation where unity-consciousness could reign once again had not yet been reached because, it would seem, the usefulness to the Creator of the dynamics of ego-separation had not yet been exhausted. As hard as it may be to understand, our ego-minds, with their drive to maintain separation, have been purposeful in the Creator's great experiment called humanity. The Creator manifested human beings with free will—the potential to develop out-of-control egos—as a way to experience duality and all the sometimes messy, horrifying ramifications thereof. We were given free will not as a mistake but as an exciting dynamic.

But the Creator also gave us the yearning to return to the ecstatic state of Oneness, and the free will to choose to do so. Only now has that desire reached the point where we have a stronger drive to embrace Oneness again than the drive to maintain separateness. The cycle of separation that started with Eve and Adam exercising their free will in a way that aligned us with the schema for disharmony is almost complete.

At last the critical mass of desire for Oneness that is needed to trigger the restoration process on a large scale has been reached. While by no means is everyone yet *consciously* on board with this, there are finally enough people who can no longer tolerate living in the misaligned world, enough awakened consciousness to comprehend the situation, and enough people who, whether they looked at it that way or not, have offered up enough of themselves to God-In-Them so that the process of recreating Paradise as a sustainable reality can progress more rapidly and easily than has ever been possible before.

For the first time since that sad day in the Garden when humans first used their free will to move *away* from God, humans are, at last, in an optimal position for using their free will to consciously and purposely initiate realignment with the Creator's Design for Harmony and Wholeness and draw as close to God as possible once again. This book is intended as a catalyst for that—a clarion call to humanity to use the gift of free will to make the choice to restore itself to Paradise. Yes, this is an auspicious time indeed.

WHAT ENSURES THAT EDEN WILL BE RECREATED, and that we will all get there, is Prime Principle, the unfailing universal law that governs all that occurs in this realm of being. Specifically, what empowers—and, indeed, guarantees—the success of this undertaking is the ingenious and infallible aspect of Prime Principle called *unified radiance*. Just as in our chapter 2 exercises with the ring magnets where the magnets increased in power and could flip other magnets around when enough of them grouped together and acted as one, unified radiance causes this effect within you, too. When even a tiny part of you intentionally aligns with the Big Magnet (God), the magnetic power of God-In-You is increased exponentially, drawing even more of you into alignment—effortlessly! Spontaneously! The more of you that is drawn into alignment, the greater the magnetic power becomes. Like dominoes, the effect continues until your restoration is complete.

This principle plays out on multiple levels simultaneously. As unified radiance works within you at a personal level, it is working at the planetary level as well. The power of your own increased magnetic force exerts pull over other aspects of Creation, including other people, bringing more and more substance into alignment. The more people, or aspects thereof, that are in alignment, the greater the magnetic power grows until, at last, *all* is drawn back into alignment.

So you see, while it affects more than just you as an individual, the process of recreating Paradise on a large scale truly does depend on what YOU do. It depends on *your* intention and *your* choices. The more you choose to obey and actively love your Spirit, thus powerfully radiating Love the way you were designed to, the more of you is in alignment. The more of you that is in alignment, the more of you is pulled into alignment! The more of you that is in alignment, the more it influences other magnets in the Whole of Creation to come into alignment, too!

So you see, it doesn't even require getting *all* of yourself on board with it. There will likely be some ego resistance even in those whose conscious minds fully see the wisdom in it. There may be parts of you so habituated to and invested in this lower-level existence that they will only come along at first kicking and screaming. "But I *like* feeling separate and I *like* stuff that keeps me at a lower frequency!" might be their hue and cry. Happily, as you surrender, unified radiance will take care of these aspects of you, too, and once you have experienced rising in frequency even a little bit, any resistant parts of you will be easily—and willingly—pulled into alignment. Believe me: however much fun you're having at the lower range of frequency, you will have far, *far* more fun in a higher one! And it is not transitory, conditional fun as we're used to, but the kind of fun that lasts.

As far as this process unfolding on a large scale goes, unified radiance makes it so that we don't have to proselytize or hit any-one over the head with it. We don't have to beat the bushes to find people to sign up for it. We simply need to *do it ourselves*. So even though the more people that commit to this, the faster the process will go, this is not about rounding up a bunch of people and saying, "This is what you have to do!" Nor do we have to have a roll call or count heads on this. Though in the larger sense, numbers count; the only number that really needs to concern you is the number *one*. There is only *one* person you need to bring on board with this—yourself. Unified radiance will handle the rest!

Of course, your Spirit certainly may prompt you to share this information with others, and if so, by all means, do. But when you share it, offer it to whomever you are guided to and then let it go. Know that those whom you are guided to share it with will recog-nize it and embrace it *when the time is right for them to* and not before. Consciousness has a way of tuning out and not being able to see what it is not ready for—what is not a frequency-match—and wholly embracing whatever it *is* ready for. That's a function of Prime Principle, of course; it's the "like attracts like" factor and it cannot be manipulated or rushed. Only your ego would want to do that anyway!

Based on the way unified radiance works, the greatest part of this process will take place at a level which we won't be able to witness, but we will certainly see clusters of people magneti-cally drawn together to accelerate the unfolding of Heaven on Earth. Indeed, there are already many of these clusters which have been drawn together for this purpose whether they see their reason for being together in these terms or not. When two or more people who are committed to recreating Heaven on Earth by their intention to operate purely in response to the guidance of their Spirits come together, the power of their union evolves the Whole of Creation.

These are synergies—combinations of energies that produce an exponential effect—an effect greater than the sum of the effects possible from each individual alone. These *evolutionary synergies* cause us to grow faster as individuals and as a whole. Though we can facilitate such synergies by making the intention to gather with others who seek to recreate Eden, the ego-mind does not have the power to create them. True evolutionary synergies are instigated by Spirit and orchestrated by unified radiance. When people are following the guidance of their Spirits, they will find themselves naturally drawn to others with whom they can truly expedite the unfolding of Heaven on Earth.

Once again, I must exclaim, "What an elegant system we have here!" All we have to do is love God completely as we were designed to do, which, of course, includes obeying our own Spirits, and Heaven on Earth will materialize spontaneously! Like the little snowball rolling downhill, picking up more and more snow and more and more speed, growing larger and going faster from only the small initial effort to form a little ball and get it rolling, unified radiance guarantees it.

Thus, the recreation of Paradise is up to you. You are a vital element in this whole thing because by your intention to do so, and by choosing to align with your Spirit—who not only embodies the blueprint for your own personal salvation but for the restoration of the Whole of Creation—*you* are the one that gets the ball rolling to expedite the restoration of humanity to the schema for harmony. You are the one who initiates the recreation of Eden for all of us.

Jesus explained this when he was planting the seeds in consciousness so long ago for the Tree of Life to flourish once more. He said, "The kingdom of heaven is like to a grain of mustard seed, which a man took, and sowed in his field which indeed is the least of all seeds: but when it is grown, it is the greatest among herbs, and becometh a tree, so that the birds of the air come and lodge in the branches thereof."[2]

Likewise, within your small, but highly significant, initial actions toward letting your Spirit take over so that Heaven can manifest for you, are contained the patterning and initiation of something far greater. You are sowing nothing less than the seeds for the Tree of Life—the Divine Design for harmony—to grow, not only in your experience, but for us all. Be assured that, like most seeds, though

---

2 Matthew 13: 31-32, *King James Version.*

they germinate and begin to grow where they cannot at first be seen, they are, indeed, growing, and will mature to become a magnificent new world.

The restoration to Eden has been slowly and quietly happening without the conscious awareness of most. Right now it is like a wave taking form far out in the ocean. What would appear to be the smallest of ripples is in actuality a powerful force gathering energy to become a mighty swell that lifts up and carries all in its path to shore. While it is true that those who don't consciously coordinate with the process in the beginning will be swept up by the wave eventually, anyway, if you are to fulfill your reason for being here now, and experience true bliss in this lifetime, not to mention if the ride is to be smooth and optimally enjoyable, it is necessary to approach this proactively and be on the leading edge of it.

BECAUSE YOUR OWN LEVEL OF FREQUENCY RAISES OR LOWERS the overall frequency, and because being at higher frequency equals the experience of joy, it is literally true that in order to raise up the world and deliver it from suffering, it is imperative that you are joyful. And most people think saving the world requires sacrifice and suffering! In fact, the very opposite is true. Indeed, the most magnanimous—and *effective* —thing you can possibly do for the planet and its inhabitants is to raise your frequency up out of pain and struggle to that of peace, joy, and ease so that the collective joy level increases, thus lifting all out of pain and struggle. What a grand plan! We are, I will reiterate, personally rewarded beyond measure for doing what needs to be done. It is built into the Creator's Design.

Now, I fully understand that joy is the last thing you may spontaneously experience when you learn of some of the perverse things that are going on here on Planet Earth, and of the distressing things that are happening in the lives of people you know and care personally for, but please understand I'm not suggesting you are to be joyful *about* the inharmonious things you see in the world; I'm saying we need to be joyful *despite* them. While this may sound cold and unfeeling, it is truly anything but.

When we go to the joy space, we lift our own frequency and, thus, the collective frequency. When we allow the horrors and sad events we observe in this world to polarize us to turmoil, fear, and sorrow, our frequency is lowered, and thus the frequency of the Whole is lowered. Allowing the inharmonious things you see occurring in the world to take you out of the joy space—or further from it—contributes to the lower-frequency energy that created it and sustains it. (Unified radiance works in the other direction, too.)

The effective response to any undesirable condition is, first and foremost, to radiate Love—the Love that comes only through correct alignment with your Spirit. This not only raises your frequency and the collective frequency, it puts you in position to receive instruction from your Spirit as to what you need to do to further lift up and change the situation in a tangible, physical way. Remember that your Spirit's omniscient guidance is available to you when you are receptive to it—something you can't be when you are receptive to circumstances.

Though the word "compassion" is rooted in the idea of feeling another's misery, *true* compassion is not demonstrated by being emotionally involved in someone's troubles. Enlightened compassion calls for you to be committed to peace and joy. Does this mean to abandon someone in times of difficulty? Absolutely not. It merely means that your job is to lift the situation up, not hang out with them at the level of the distress or focus on the distress, thus adding more energy to it. Real, useful compassion is recognizing when someone is suffering because of a lower frequency event or condition and then to build a vibrational bridge upward for them.

Thus, when you become aware of someone in distress, make a point to feel the immense Love from your Spirit filling you up, and allow the Love response to bring you into the realm of peace and joy. Then, mentally and emotionally, bring the one or ones in distress into that space with you to lift them up. This is what compassion truly is—not jumping into the sadness or stress with them and thus lowering everyone's frequency, but providing a vibrational lifeline that can help to move them out of distress and closer to joy, too.

I realize that until you are more consistently dwelling at a higher frequency, it can be a challenge to go from an awareness of what is going on in the misaligned world—especially if it is something that is touching you or someone you care about—straight up in frequency to the joy space. However, it is possible to at least feel peace—the peace of alignment with your Spirit—despite any circumstance. Simply release it to your Spirit to lift it up. The point is to bring yourself into proper response so that you can raise the frequency level of all instead of adding to the disharmony by investing passion in it.

It is important to stay attuned with your feeling nature in this process, even while you are refusing to be embroiled in the distress. As feeling beings, we register energy with our emotions. When emotions are triggered, it is important to allow the energy that activated them to move on through, be it through crying or other emotional release. While your goal is to increase your tenure in the realm of joy, clearing out any less-than-joyful feelings that arise in you *as they arise* is vital. To block them is to lower your frequency. Energy must be able to move freely through you to keep your frequency high. Allowing emotional energy to express and then letting it move along *without getting caught up in it* frees you to be joyful and at peace. You can't be fully joyful or peaceful when the vibrational weight of trapped emotions is weighing you down.

IN THE PROCESS OF RENOVATING OUR LIVES, and thus, the glorious home we call Earth, things may at times appear to be a big mess, both up close and globally. Just as when a house is remodeled, a certain amount of disarray—even apparent chaos—is bound to ensue before the new, improved structure emerges. If you don't know what is going on, you might see the remodeling mess as a sign of disaster. But when you *do* know the plan, you are aware that the mess is simply a part of the process of creating something new and more desirable. The way we can most efficiently remodel our home and stay unfazed and unaffected by the chaos is by holding steady and refusing to buy into the illusion that something is going wrong.

Though it is true that *only peace, joy, and harmony* exist when you are operating at the frequency of your Spirit, and though it is true that your life experience will improve dramatically by simply beginning to hand your life over to your Spirit, you may encounter some turbulence along the way. Even though your experience of joy will increase as you rise in frequency, and your experience of those things that manifest at lower frequencies will diminish, you must remember that recreating Eden is a *process,* and while instantaneous transformation is certainly possible, disentangling from the schema for disharmony may not be without times of challenge. Indeed, you may find that rising up to close the magnetic gap brings with it a mix of joy and, shall we say, "less-than-joy." (But definitely more of the former than the latter!)

As long as you are an amalgam of magnets in alignment and magnets out of alignment, there will be some degree of turmoil present in you—but not nearly as much or as pervasively as before you began allowing your Spirit to restore your life. I would be remiss, though, if I did not caution you that increasing your frequency might bring with it some symptoms to get through before you reach the point where you have completely left conflict and pain behind to dwell in continuous harmony and peace. To put it in coarse terms, it can really stir up your "stuff."

While this is definitely a sign of progress, it sure may not seem that way when you're in the midst of it! Adding more pure Light— more Life Force—by intentionally merging with your Spirit is sure to displace the lower frequency energy and the manifestations thereof in your being. And when that gunk is stirred up and in the process of realigning and clearing, sometimes it can block the Light from your awareness. It can deepen the shadows in your consciousness so that if you are not aware and prepared, it can *appear* that things are going wrong. Do not be fooled!

Just remember that as the shadows deepen, they do so because they only exist by virtue of the Light. The deepest shadows in the physical world are created by being adjacent to the brightest light— and so it is with this process. When your stuff comes up, it is something to celebrate—it is a sign that the Light within you has increased—even if it doesn't look or feel much like it in the moment! The more you can go through such times without getting emotionally caught up in them, and avoid buying into the illusion that the Light is gone, the faster you will move upward and out of it, and the easier it will be.

To get through the rough times, you need to withdraw your energy and focus from the darkness and invest it in the Light. Fighting, or even simply resisting, the shadows only empowers them. If you get emotionally or psychologically caught up in the shadow stuff, you lower your frequency, enabling the darkness to continue. Focusing your attention on the shadow, or giving any passion to it at all, aligns you with it instead of with your Spirit. The shadow remains because it has found a frequency match—a way to be fed with energy, something every entity needs to be able to exist. Remember: don't feed the serpent!

As you focus your attention on the Light instead—on your Spirit—you withdraw energy from the shadows of reverse polarity and increase the Light. There is only one way to get rid of a shadow. You must flood it with Light. And of course, you do that by continually surrendering to and loving your Spirit. Even when the Light *seems* to be eluding you, cling to your Spirit as if It were a life buoy—It is. As you do, such challenging times will occur less and less until they disappear altogether. In the meantime, I can assure you that your overall increased harmony, joy, and peace will more than make up for any patches of difficulty you may encounter on the way to the trouble-free zone we're calling "Eden!"

WHEN I STUMBLED THROUGH THE GARDEN GATE THAT AMAZING DAY in Switzerland, I had no awareness whatever of frequency, of unified radiance, of an energy hierarchy, of my Original Self, or even that Paradise was an accessible state. I had no clue what I was moving toward—I was simply, albeit out of desperation at first, following my Spirit's guidance to get out of the pain I was in. The more obedient I was, the greater the rewards. The more I felt the Love from my Spirit and loved my Spirit in response, the more joyful I became!

As I let go to the upward surge of my energy, which I now

understand was my frequency rising, even the most difficult problems were solved like magic. The pain that once ruled my life subsided dramatically and, in a short time, was gone altogether. Even in those early months before Switzerland, before I was able to do all that my Spirit had guided me to do to heal myself—even when my body was still manifesting symptoms that were potentially horrifying—I was so immersed in my new Love-relationship with my Spirit that I was above it all and experiencing immense joy despite the condition my body was in. Of course, once I was able to do the physical things that needed to be done and I rose even higher in frequency, the physical symptoms vanished, too.

I didn't bother to analyze it then, but I now understand that what I experienced was exactly the predictable response. As we rise up in frequency, we enter the vibrational realm of our Spirits. In this realm, joy is the emotional response to that frequency spectrum; disease, pain, and suffering do not even exist there! So just like Paradise doesn't exist until you are at a certain frequency, lower-frequency experiences such as illness, pain, and sorrow do not exist unless you are operating at *their* frequency. The higher your frequency, the less possible it is for lower-frequency experiences to manifest for you, as you are no longer an energy match.

Though you can leave that higher-vibrational realm and return to a lower frequency where you can once again embrace suffering and less-than-joy if you choose to, when you are in the frequency range of your Spirit, there is no such thing. There is only ease, joy, and peace. Peace prevails at the higher frequencies your Spirit inhabits because *peace is a function of perfect magnetic alignment*. When all magnets are in perfect alignment, the conflict that occurs between energies moving in different directions just doesn't exist!

As you climb higher in frequency, close the magnetic gap, and bring all that is under your dominion in the energy hierarchy up with you as a result, the only energy that is a match with you is of higher frequency, too. Therefore, anything that isn't a frequency match simply drops off your radar and ceases to exist for you! They are no longer a part of your reality. You literally *leave them behind.* Your new reality is one of only higher-frequency energies. In this sense, you can say that you actually *do* escape the trials of Earth-life and "go to another place" as you approach Eden.

Not only will everyone and everything vibrating at a frequency below your frequency range disappear from your awareness, you will disappear from theirs! Just as Eden cannot be seen from the level where most Earth-dwellers currently operate, neither can the residents of Eden. Once you reach a certain vibrational level, you will seem to have vanished to those vibrating significantly lower than that!

Even now, as your internal magnets are realigning, there are parts of you operating at a higher frequency, and those aspects of you may as well not even exist from the vantage point of lower frequency. You may have had the sensation before of someone in your physical sphere being utterly unaware of you or of parts of you. This is because that part of you is virtually invisible to them. This can be particularly disconcerting to your ego. (I say this from personal experience!) But when you let more and more of yourself be absorbed by your Spirit, it will not be a problem at all—after all, your ego will be vanishing, too!

Happily, this works the other way around as well. As you rise in frequency, those parts of other people vibrating at a lower frequency than is a frequency match for you will seem to disappear as well, and the parts of them vibrating at the higher frequency that matches yours will be enhanced in your awareness. It will seem to you as if everyone is more delightful when you rise in frequency! If you've ever heard the advice "You can't change anyone else, you can only change yourself," this is the ultimate manifestation of that! (Of course, by changing yourself, unified radiance will change them, but till then, it's nice to know about this other aspect of the process and how it affects your perceptions!)

As you approach Eden, anyone who is within your frequency range will remain a part of your life, and anyone who is not will cease being a part of your reality—until they rise in frequency. Remember, *everyone* will be coming along in time due to the awesome power of unified radiance—but only those who have surrendered to their Spirits and dropped their baggage can make it through the Garden's security system, and it will take some of us longer than others. So worry not. This does not mean you will experience a permanent distancing from loved ones, but it will change your relationship and may mean being without them—or at least a full consciousness of them—temporarily. However, it will not be a problem. Your whole perception of things—of time, of distance, of separation and connection—is about to change, and I can promise you when the time comes, you will not be the least bit concerned. Think of it as going on ahead to Paradise to prepare for their arrival so that you can all have a wonderful time when they get there!

This process will bring delightful, amazing surprises, and some of them may include the seemingly magical, unexpected transformations of people you would have sworn could never turn around so quickly! And yes, even people you may currently dislike will be in Eden, too, but worry not—they can't get there as long as they are operating contrary to the Divine Design for harmony and wholeness. (Nor can you!) Once you are in the frequency range of Eden, everyone you meet there will have escaped the bonds of reverse polarity and will be in harmony. By the time you reach the higher levels of frequency, you will hold no rancor toward anyone nor will anyone feel enmity for you—indeed, such attitudes won't make it through the security system! When you're in Oneness, remember, there is no judgment at all—only Love.

Imagine—Heaven on Earth. A world where Love prevails, and real happiness is not something you long for, but is the foundation of your existence. Imagine a world in which no one is motivated to harm another, no one suffers, no one has to do anything that is against his or her true nature, and where everyone is free to be infinitely creative and follow their enthusiasm. Imagine a world of fulfillment and unending pleasure. If it sounds almost *too* perfect—even a little dull—just you wait! By the time you draw close to the Garden, you will see that such perfection is exactly what you—and the rest of us—were designed for, and that a whole new universe of excitement is opening up for you—a realm of infinite fascinations that you couldn't even fathom before, let alone access. You won't miss the old lower-level stuff *at all*.

WOW. WE ARE RECREATING EDEN! Can you feel the excitement? Since Adam and Eve left there so very long ago, this has been the elusive dream for humanity: the pure harmony, exquisite simplicity, boundless joy, and enduring peace of Home. These have been in our collective psyche since the beginning. We have longed for them, quested for them, begged God for them, and, in our ignorance, even fought wars for them, but these heavenly qualities have remained out of our collective reach. Not anymore.

No longer is our true home to be just vague memories and a mythical quest—it is to be our very reality. From this frightening world where violence, greed, cruelty, deceit, suffering, and filth are rampant, we are rising up to a world where these perversions of Love cannot even exist, much less affect us. Where we are headed, pure Love holds sovereign power and radiates from us as brightly as light from the sun. In this sparkling fresh world we are creating, *all* is restored to the original design of harmony and wholeness, and our remarkable Earth is free to become the shining star she was intended to be.

I hope you now see why you are here. I hope you now understand who you really are and what you are here to do. I hope you now understand how you, the hero of your own story, is saved! I hope you see how simple and possible it is. I hope you realize how joyous the trip home is going to be. I hope you are as excited as I am over the prospect of returning to Paradise! And most of all, I hope you will now join me in recreating Eden. The dream is in reach. Our beautiful new world is calling us home.

In case I don't see you on the way, I'll meet you there!

A Preview of Eden

*H*ERE IS A CREATIVE ACTIVITY YOU CAN USE TO GET A "SNEAK PEEK" OF YOUR ARRIVAL IN EDEN. Using all your senses, as well as your capacity to create various sensations in your body and turn on joy, you can elevate your frequency upward toward Home by utilizing your creativity tool kit, which includes, among other qualities: play, imagination, possibility thinking, faith, wholeheartedness, and present-time awareness, to imagine and *feel* attaining the vibrational frequency of Eden.

While I believe you can benefit from just reading this and responding according to the cues in it with your eyes open, you might find it helpful to have a partner read it to you or to read it aloud slowly into a tape recorder, allowing time in between each part for you to visualize and experience it, so you can play it back for yourself and follow along with your eyes closed to enhance the potency of it. (If you do this, you might want to put it in first person, changing "you" to "I" and "your" to "my.")

Your Spirit may guide you to imagine something more, or something different, and of course, you are free to modify this in any way you feel led to. As always, follow your Spirit above all else!

The experience begins as you are awakening from a long, deep sleep . . .

As your consciousness comes into focus, you realize that something—everything—has shifted. You marvel at the rising excitement and anticipation you are experiencing for no apparent reason. Not since you were a young child have you felt such giddiness in just being alive. You are so filled with happiness, you are about to burst with it!

Going forth, you become aware of something unprecedented—there is only beauty surrounding you! The pristine air is fragranced with the most beautiful, clean scent you have ever encountered, and the aroma of your favorite flower wafts in and out of your awareness. The light is brighter and clearer, yet gentler and more embracing. As if she has taken a shower of crystalline energy, Mother Earth is glowing and glorious, pulsating with Love, and you feel overwhelming Love pouring forth from you to her. All around you, Nature dances in celebration as you feel yourself rising higher and higher.

As feather light as you feel, it seems there are butterflies in your cells, lifting you off the ground. A smile is encompassing your whole being, and you are the personification of joy. Everyone you encounter is radiant as well, and you know without asking that they are experiencing the same bliss you are. The harmony you are feeling with everyone and everything is new—yet familiar. Your expanding heart opens like a blossom in the morning sun, and the boundaries that once separated you dissolve.

You know Oneness. You know Who You Are. As this awareness explodes in your consciousness, wave after wave of ecstasy cascades through your body and Love radiates from you to bless all Creation.

Fully embraced in the Heart of God, the world of your experience is reborn and all is as it was always meant to be. You have arrived at last! You are Home.

Welcome back to Eden.

ACKNOWLEDGMENTS

$\mathcal{T}$HIS PROJECT, WHILE *WRITTEN* SOLELY BY ME, WAS HARDLY A SOLO EFFORT. It could not have been birthed without the support, both emotional and physical, of a wonderful team of family, friends, and publishing professionals. I must credit as well, my many teachers, whether they understood that's what they were to me or not, both on the Earth plane and beyond, for helping me develop my talents and evolve in consciousness to the place where I could manifest this material.

Primarily, thank you, my Spirit, for guiding me throughout my life, for your immense direct role in getting this book manifested, and, of course, for showing me Eden.

No person has demonstrated more faith in this project, or in me, than my husband, Rick, who, with his constant encouragement (and breadwinning!), has "supported the arts" so that I could be free, both time-wise and psychologically, to birth this baby we've named *Recreating Eden*. My dear Rick: Your abiding confidence in me and this project, your many pep talks, your "comma doctoring," and your steadfast refusal to knuckle under to practical concerns that might have made another spouse beg me to "get a *real* job" have earned you a place in the Partnership Hall of Fame. That I found a mate who is such a loyal supporter and great friend, who loves me as much as you do, and whom I love to the depths of my soul, *and* who is on the same spiritual wavelength with me, is a miracle that never ceases to amaze me! Thank you for being—and for being with me.

My dearest stepdaughters: I am grateful to your dad for sharing you with me, and to you for sharing your love, energy, and joy. You'll never know how many times during the writing of this book, I was bogged down in thinking too much, and you guys showed up and shifted the energy. Thank you for the pure fun and delight you bring!

Thank you, Mom and Dad, for your immense unconditional love and support. I know you haven't always understood me or my path, but you have always been eager to do all you could to support whatever I wanted to do. It is empowering to know that I am loved in that way. Ann and Linda, my always-supportive sisters: I appreciate you, for a host of reasons, more than you will ever know.

To the rest of my wonderful family and many longtime friends: I thank you for believing in me even when you didn't have much of a clue what specific task I was up to with my writing, or when I would ever have anything to show for my years of work. How I do so appreciate your blind faith in me! Please know that I did not share more of the details sooner because it was important not to spread the energy too thin—and to be honest, for a long time, I didn't know the details myself! You are too numerous to list, but I know *you know who you are.*

To my enthusiastic "cheerleaders," Brenda Williams and dd, I offer deep gratitude for believing in this project and holding steady in your convictions about its importance, even during those times when I found it a challenge to.

Sherry Roberts, I thank you for your great work in putting this manuscript into a palatable form with your beautiful interior design, proofreading, and typesetting, and for your help in improving my cover design and making it printable. But even more than that, I thank you for being excited about this, my baby, and for treating it with such respect.

Thank you, Stevie Wonder, for providing the "soundtrack to this book." What a gift to the planet you are! Countless times I listened to *Songs In the Key of Life* to shoot me right up to the level where I could meet higher Truth and ground it into words. What waves of gratitude and Love for Spirit your music evokes in me! Specifically, "I Am Singing," "If It's Magic," and "As" helped me get in touch with the rhythm of life and with my joy so that I could give life to the message of *Recreating Eden*.

And last, thank you, my precious canine companions, Roly and Lilah, and, of course, the others who, though they have completed their Earth-sojourn with me, are always with me in Spirit. Without your uncomplicated devotion, freely offered pure Love, and your infinite capacity to receive Love from me, I would find Earth—in any stage of evolution—a far less hospitable place.

Julia Rogers Hamrick

Wishing for some extra companionship for the trip Home?

Be on the lookout for

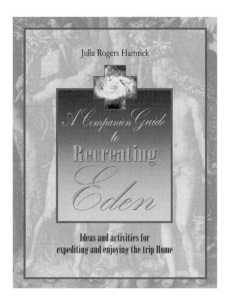

A Companion Guide to Recreating Eden is designed to support and enhance your process of aligning with your Spirit to transform your world. With ideas and activities that help you expand on what you discovered in *Recreating Eden,* this learning tool from author and spiritual-growth facilitator **Julia Rogers Hamrick** will assist you in staying focused, keeping your energy moving, and growing in joy!

Find out more at www.recreating-eden.com

For news of activities relating to **Recreating Eden**

To sign up for the free **Recreating Eden**
e-mail newsletter

For free, downloadable **Recreating Eden**
book-study guides

be sure to visit

www.recreating-eden.com

To give the gift of **Recreating Eden,** or to
purchase copies for your book-study group, check
your local bookstore or www.recreating-eden.com.